Developmental Classroom Guidance Activities

By Susan E. Ferbert, M.Ed.
Deborah A. Griffith, M.A.
& Donna B. Forrest, Ed.S.

©2000 by
YouthLight, Inc.
Chapin, SC 29036

Cover Design & Layout by Elizabeth Madden
Project Editing by Susan Bowman & Renee Reasinger

ISBN-1-889636-33-9

Library of Congress Number
00-191129

10 9 8 7 6 5 4 3 2 1
Printed in the United States

YouthLight, Inc.
P.O. Box 115 • Chapin, South Carolina 29036
(800) 209-9774 • (803) 345-1070
Fax (803) 345-0888 • Email YLDR1@aol.com
www.youthlight.com

Dedication

Susan S. Ferbert dedicates this book in loving memory of her father, and the continual love and support from her mother. She also wants to acknowledge Bob Bowman for mentoring and encouraging her to write, as well as close friends and family who have provided emotional and intellectual support throughout the writing of this book.

Deborah A. Griffith wishes to dedicate this book to her loving husband, Jeremy Griffith, who patiently and selflessly supported her throughout the writing. Deborah also wants to acknowledge her parents who have always encouraged her to pursue her educational interests. Thanks to Sue Ferbert, too, for encouraging me to take this opportunity.

Donna B. Forrest would like to dedicate this book personally to her children Derek, and April and the teens constantly in and out of her home, all of whom, model and teach her excellent character lessons! And, professionally to the staff of Merriwether Elementary School, Community Care and Counseling of North Augusta, and First Baptist Church of North Augusta – all of who display and advocate for good character with numerous children, adolescents and adults on a day-to-day basis.

Acknowledgments

We would like to thank the following people who contributed to this book:

Kim Dupre who submitted not only ideas, but lessons for our first unit.

Ginny Silski who helped develop and fine tune ideas.

Jen Dework and Joel Katz who provided information on tools for mountain climbing.

Steve Markwood and Richard Gaylord for ideas on artwork depicting perspectives.

Terri Whiddon who contributed information regarding how to play the game "Mother May I?"

Suzie Taylor for helping gather sources on the circus.

Jeremy Griffith who helped field test some of our activities.

Elizabeth Madden and Renee Reasinger from YouthLight, Inc. for their creative ideas and layout.

To Sue Ferbert and Deborah Griffith, Donna Forrest would like to acknowledge their patience in waiting on the final chapters.

To all Middle School teachers and staff members who so diligently work for hours each day to improve the quality of life for children at such a difficult developmental level.

Table of Contents

> *"A musician must make music, an artist must paint, a poet must write, if he is to be ultimately at peace with himself. What a man can be, he must be."*
>
> \- Abraham Harold Maslow

Welcome friends:

The philosophy upon which this book is based is Abraham Maslow's hierarchy of needs. Maslow proposed that humans have certain basic needs of survival and safety. After having those needs met, then people are free to move to a level where intellectual needs are met.

Opponents of Maslow say that they do not believe that learning takes place in a straight line, but rather that people move up and down through basic and higher level needs and may work on more than one need at a time. (Woolfolk, 1995).

Regardless of how students work through needs, students struggle with unmet needs, which interfere with their ability to learn at a maximum level. "We are just beginning, however, to appreciate the many new pressures society now imposes on children - pressures that previous generations of children never knew" (Moorefield, 1984).

The goal of this book is to overlap the boundaries between counseling and teaching, for the purpose of reaching as many students as possible and by providing greater emotional guidance to lead students toward a healthy emotional independence. By teaming up teachers and counselors, students can be reached on a more consistent and timely basis.

We hope you find this book helpful whether you are a teacher, counselor, or both, and regardless of your amount of experience. The activities have been field-tested, revised, and polished to effectively meet students' needs. Designed to assist counselors and teachers in presenting creative group and classroom counseling lessons, it has been geared for students in grades four through eight, but may be adapted to higher or lower grades as needed.

As a former teacher and current counselors, we are always looking for creative new methods to present ideas. As professionals, it is often difficult to meet the diversity of needs of such large caseloads. Therefore by designing lessons that can be taught jointly by teachers and counselors, we are expanding our capabilities and reaching more students on a consistent basis. Teachers, by participating as facilitators of these lessons, will be able to meet the emotional needs of their students on a greater or more well rounded basis. Therefore, students will be ready to learn and function more efficiently in settings which present high expectations.

By presenting lessons, which actively engage students, we have naturally opened a door to encourage students to internally value emotional independence and development.

Many of the lessons in this book incorporate standard academic learning expectations for various subjects in grades four through eight. Thus this program provides an integrated approach; combining academic and developmental guidance goals within the same lesson.

Our ideas came from our personal experiences with our university counselor education programs and our experiences in the public schools following our formal training. We have consulted with university professors and other school counselors with varying levels of experience. We also studied other exemplary middle school counseling programs. Ideas have also come from resources made available through our counties of employment and our communities. Workshops and professional development have further added to our knowledge and skills. The rest was left to basic instinct and ideas, personal research, and life experiences.

Although we have spent many hours putting together and trying the ideas enclosed in this book, we would greatly appreciate hearing any comments, ideas, suggestions, or questions. We can be reached at the e-mail address listed below. We will try to promptly respond to questions.

e-mail address: developmentalact@hotmail.com

Thank you for choosing our book. We hope it strengthens your counseling and teaching programs!

Chapter 1

Responsible Behavior

"Intelligence is quickness to apprehend as distinct from ability, which is capacity to act wisely on the thing apprehended."

- Alfred North Whitehead

The goal of this unit on responsible behavior is to help students independently make wise choices. The unit focuses on self-monitoring and self-directing. Lessons include information on identifying characteristics of responsible behavior, clarifying when behaviors are appropriate, looking at thoughts associated with behaviors, and the decision making process.

Positive Pals

Objectives

Students will:

✔ characterize effective and ineffective behavior in and out of the classroom setting

✔ practice cooperative learning skills and techniques

✔ gain a greater sense of self-esteem

✔ identify positive ways to deal with situations they will endure in and out of school

Materials Needed

3x5 index cards for role plays
Pen or pencil

Procedures

1. Explain that this will be an activity in which all students will have a chance to participate in and give their ideas and opinions.

2. Pair students into groups of two, preferably with students they do not know as well. This will provoke them to get to know others and learn how to initiate conversations.

3. Give each pair a 3x5 index card and ask them to come up with a conflict that they have dealt with during school with other students, or at home (Example: A student is being ridiculed by another student).

4. Each pair writes down on the index card a couple of sentences explaining the conflict.

5. Give each pair about 10-15 minutes to role play the event, each playing both sides. They must have one partner acting out an effective way in dealing with the situation, as well as the other partner acting out a less effective way.

6. Each group is asked to come up to the front and demonstrate both reactions to their situations. The rest of the class is called upon to decide which reaction is the most effective behavior, and what other reactions they would consider to be suitable.

7. Extend this activity for a month, with students having new partners each week in order to learn how to work with peers.

Discussion Questions

1. What were the reasons you were paired with students other than your friends?
2. What did you learn from listening and watching your peers' conflicts?
3. How do you determine whether your behavior is considered effective?
4. How do you determine whether a behavior is not effective?
5. Can you name one positive thing you gained from participating in this activity?

Variations

Positive Pals can be varied in several ways. Role plays can be devised and passed out to the students. Role plays can be fictitious or situations they have had to deal with at school or at home. Students may practice role plays outside of class, and bring in props to act out the plays including puppets. Role plays may be done in a private setting with individual students who are quieter. Also students may sketch behaviors to situations. The class can devise questions to be asked after the activity has been completed. The activity may be tailored for any time length (Example: a week, a month, etc.). After students have practiced techniques, challenge them by presenting them with an impromptu conflict without time to rehearse.

Date_____

Dear Parent/Guardian:

Today in class students participated in the "Positive Pals" activity, which works well with students of all ages, for it teaches them how to cooperate with others in school and at home. Students were paired with other peers and role played effective and ineffective responses to common conflicts they may encounter in school or at home.

Students are constantly being faced with new situations, which are a part of life. There is always more than one choice in a given situation. The quality of their life is dependent upon their ability to choose the most effective option for them.

Naturally you want to see your child succeed. Encourage your child to get to know him/herself. This can be accomplished by providing an opportunity to make choices. Role plays give your child a chance to make choices. They can be planned and acted out, or children can be asked to stop when they are in a real life event and asked to think how they should effectively deal with the situation. Children can learn at home how to more effectively deal with conflicts and situations that arise with other siblings, with parents, and with people in general. As a role model you also play an important part in your child's life. Keep up the effective decision making!

Sincerely,

_____

Cartoon Behaviors

<table>
<tr><td>

Objectives

Students will:

✔ discuss the possibility that there is more than one feeling a person can have about an event

✔ choose thoughts which correspond with the feeling

</td><td>

Materials Needed

Cartoons (Master attached)
Paper
Pencil
Chalkboard
Chalk

</td></tr>
</table>

Procedures

1. Present students with possible situations regularly faced by students.
   Examples: You receive a "C" on a test.
   Someone bumps into you in the hall and you drop all your books.
   You work a problem on the board and get a wrong answer.

2. Give students time to independently write what they would feel after facing the given situation.

3. List on the board, feelings of each student to the given situation and discuss thoughts about each feeling.
   Example Situation: You receive a "C" on a test
   Possible Feelings: Happy, Angry, Disappointed
   Thought associated with each feeling:

Happy:	I really did well.
	I studied hard and it paid off.
	I did my best. A "C" is okay, it is average.
	This is not my best, but next time I'll do better.
Angry:	I'm so stupid.
	Everyone else got an "A."
	This test wasn't fair. The teacher didn't teach us this stuff.
Disappointed:	I wish I would have done better.
	I usually do better, but I was really busy.

4. Pass out the cartoons to students working in groups.

5. Have students write in possible thoughts and feelings associated with each situation.

6. Share and discuss thoughts and feelings toward the situations represented in the graphics.

Discussion Questions

1. Why are there different feelings to the same event?
2. Are feelings ever "right" or "wrong?"
3. To whom do the feelings belong?
4. What can you do if you're experiencing an unpleasant feeling?
5. Within your group, what thoughts occurred frequently?
6. What is the difference between a thought and a feeling?

Variations

• Have students sketch alternate cartoons for alternate thoughts and feelings to same situation.
• Have students keep a weekly log of events or situations that occur to them. Have them list thoughts and feelings regarding event.
• Have students brainstorm a list of thoughts which are likely to produce "positive" emotions.

Cartoon Behaviors

Situation-You thought of a possible solution for how to remember your locker combination.

Feeling:_____

Thought: _____

_____

_____

Situation-Someone was making noises and the teacher blamed you.

Feeling:_____

Thought: _____

_____

_____

Situation-You were chosen as student of the month.

Feeling:_____

Thought: _____

_____

_____

Situation-Someone just called you "Fattie."

Feeling:_____

Thought: _____

_____

_____

Situation-You were chosen for the lead role in the school play.

Feeling:_____

Thought: _____

_____

_____

Situation-Everyone else is finished, but you're still not sure where to begin.

Feeling:_____

Thought: _____

_____

_____

Cartoon Behaviors

Situation-You worked a math problem on the board and got an incorrect answer.

Feeling:_____

Thought: _____

_____

_____

Situation-You just won a wrestling match.

Feeling:_____

Thought: _____

_____

_____

Situation-You were telling the class a joke and got confused. The joke came out all confused and incorrect.

Feeling:_____

Thought: _____

_____

_____

Date_____

Dear Parent/Guardian:

In the activity "Cartoon Behaviors" your child examined feelings that correspond to given situations. We discussed how two people who experience the same event can have two different reactions or feelings regarding that event. Students identified the thoughts that corresponded to the feeling expressed.

By understanding the connection between thoughts and feelings, students are given the power to understand or manage how they feel. As a result your child can choose to have sunny days more often!

You have created a warm and loving environment for your child. Communication can keep this warmth and love flowing. You may want to discuss with your child the events he/she is experiencing and his/her feelings about those events. Ask your child to state the thoughts he/she is having regarding the situation or event.

Sincerely,

_____

Decision Making for All

Objectives

Students will:

✔ make decisions for given problems.

✔ list steps for the decision making process.

✔ create a method to easily teach second-graders the steps to decision making.

Materials Needed

Scenario handouts
Available classroom objects to stimulate creativity. (Possible items: poster board, markers, crayons, glue, keyboard, guitar, thesaurus, glitter, clay, construction paper, paper bags, cloth, etc.)

Procedures

1. Ask students how many of them have ever made a decision before. Then ask how many of them have made a decision they wish they would have made differently. Explain to students that we are all faced with decisions and we will be sharpening our decision making skills today.

2. Pass out the sheet listing the scenarios.

3. Explain to students that they are to make a decision using the given scenarios.

4. Read and discuss the scenario sheet briefly.

5. Put students in groups, as they make a decision, have them list the steps they took to reach the decision.

6. Allow each group to discuss the steps they used.

7. Generate a list of steps for the entire class. Possible steps may include the following: Identify the problem, brainstorm possible solutions, evaluate solutions and consequences of each, choose a solution, implement chosen solutions, evaluate.

8. Explain to students that they are going to come up with an easy way to help second-grade students learn the steps to decision making. It may be necessary to discuss with students the need to keep steps simple and clear. Encourage students to be creative and fun.

9. Make supplies available to students.

10. Put students in groups and allow them to brainstorm ways to teach. As they work, rotate around the room and offer encouragement and assistance as needed.

11. Taking turns, allow each group to present its ideas to the entire group.

12. You may choose to allow students to take their ideas and teach them to a group of second graders.

Discussion Questions

1. What is the value in effective decision making?
2. When is it most difficult to make wise decisions?
3. What is the most important step in decision making?
4. How do most people learn to make wise decisions?
5. When is a time you could have benefited from the decision making process information?
6. What is the best decision you ever made and did you use any of the steps?

Variations

- Video the students teaching the decision making process and allow other teachers to show the film in their classrooms.
- As a whole group, brainstorm ways to teach the steps, then let smaller groups select an idea from the large group's brainstorming session.
- Have students record a decision they made, listing each step of the process.
- Put students in group. Assign each group one step in the decision-making process and have each group then develop a way to teach the particular step. Put all the steps together.

Decision Making for All

"Scenarios" Handout

You forgot your key to your house at home today. It is thirty-five degrees outside. When you get home no one else will be there. What do you do?

_____

_____

_____

_____

_____

_____

_____

_____

_____

_____

A friend starts calling you negative names and makes insulting comments about you and your family. He/she then stops talking to you. What will you do?

_____

_____

_____

_____

_____

_____

_____

_____

_____

Date_____

Dear Parent/Guardian:

In "Decision Making for All" your child developed a list of formal steps for making wise decisions, and formulated a method for teaching these steps to second-graders.

There is a time for all of us when decisions need to be made, and some may be more difficult than others. It is for these difficult times that your child has learned the decision making process.

As they use this process it will become easier for them to make decisions. We continue to learn to build and perfect our decision making skills.

Support your child as he/she grows in his/her decision making skills by providing opportunities to use these skills. Begin by discussing the decisions he/she is currently facing. As your child begins to make the decision, ask him/her to list each step of the process and to share with you the procedure for progressing through the steps. We hope your child will make the best decision possible.

Sincerely,

_____

Dear Diary

Objectives

Students will:

✔ discuss classroom goals and rules

✔ discuss appropriate and inappropriate classroom behavior

✔ correctly log behavior in corresponding notebook

Materials Needed

Two Notebooks (with each student's name written on one page in each book)

Procedures

1. Discuss classroom goals or rules.

2. Define and discuss appropriate and inappropriate behaviors.

3. Give examples of behaviors and ask students if they are appropriate or inappropriate.

4. Show students the notebooks and explain the purpose and procedure for use of each.

5. Throughout the week each student monitors his/her behavior. Students record in the corresponding notebook whether that behavior was appropriate or inappropriate.

6. At the end of the week, randomly choose inappropriate behaviors that have been displayed. Ask the class to brainstorm ways the inappropriate behavior could be changed to an appropriate behavior.

7. Ask students who have had no or few inappropriate behaviors logged for the week to discuss how they choose to act appropriately.

Discussion Questions

1. When is it most difficult to follow class rules?
2. How do you feel about logging your behaviors?
3. What things can you do to prevent having an inappropriate behavior?
4. What behaviors do you consider to be appropriate?
5. How would you react to a friend who is displaying inappropriate behavior?
6. Before choosing a behavior, what questions can you ask yourself to help make a wise choice?

Variations

- Allow younger students who can not write to draw their behaviors.
- Students may be placed on teams and given points or rewards for positive behaviors.
- Take students to a common area of the building that is currently being used by other students.
- Have your students identify appropriate and inappropriate behaviors exhibited by the other group of students.

Date_____

Dear Parent/Guardian:

Students told their deepest secrets concerning their behavior in the "Dear Diary" activity. We discussed our classroom rules, and what were appropriate and inappropriate behaviors. We also learned how to log appropriate and inappropriate behaviors in notebooks. Students will be learning how to monitor their own behavior.

The first step to changing any behavior is awareness. For those students who are on task and show appropriate behaviors this provides an opportunity for praise. Other students may need to set some goals and obtain behavioral objectives.

Your behavioral model has set an example for your child to follow. At various points in time ask your child how he/she views his/her behavior and why. Begin to teach your child to give positive feedback and to set realistic expectations. If your child is not pleased with his/her behavior you may ask him/her why and question how it may be changed. Your positive behavioral model will lead your child to make the wisest choices.

Sincerely,

_____

Red Light, Green Light

Objectives

Students will:

✔ pause, when necessary, prior to reacting to stimulus or situation

✔ identify helpful questions to consider to make a wise choice about a given circumstance

Material Needed

"Situations" sheet

Procedures

1. Read to students a situation and the given choice responses.

2. Assign an area of the room to correlate with response "a", another part of room to correlate to response "b", and a third part to correlate to response "c."

3. Students will stand in the area of the room that corresponds to the reaction with which they are most comfortable. Those students who are having a hard time deciding where to stand, will stand in the center of the room (this is considered the red light, because they need to "stop" and think).

4. Ask students in the corners of the room to generate helpful questions persons can ask themselves to make wise decisions. (Examples: What do I want to happen?, What is most important to me?, What will the consequence of my actions be?).

5. Have someone from each corner discuss his/her decision.

6. Read the next question, and have students repeat the process.

Discussion Questions

1. Who can discuss a time when he/she needed to "stop" and think about a decision?
2. What signs does your body give you that indicate you need to stop and think?
3. What emotions do you feel when you need to take time to think?
4. Did anyone consider where his/her friends were standing when making a choice?
5. Was anyone the only person who made a particular choice and how did that feel?
6. What is a possible "red light situation" you may encounter?

Variations

- Allow students to create situations and brainstorm possible solutions.
- In groups, allow students to dramatize or sketch the signs their bodies give to indicate they are uncomfortable with a decision.
- Students may indicate choice by raising their hands.

Red Light, Green Light

"Situations" Sheet

1. You have math homework and a paper due tomorrow, but your favorite television show is coming on television. What do you do?
   a) You do your homework
   b) You watch television
   c) You do neither

2. You have been grounded by your parents, but a group of your friends invites you to go to the mall with them.
   a) You stay home.
   b) You go to the mall.
   c) You do neither

3. You are asked to go to the school dance by a person who you do not find interesting.
   a) You go to the dance with the boy/girl.
   b) You stay home.
   c) You go to the dance without the boy/girl who asked you.

4. Your friends have the keys to their mother's car and want you to go for a spin with them. Their mother does not know they have the keys.
   a) You go with them.
   b) You do not go with them.
   c) You inform their mother of the situation.

5. You have a report due tomorrow. You have not started the report. A friend tells you he/she can get you a report off the internet on your topic.
   a) You take him/her up on the offer.
   b) You start your own report immediately.
   c) You don't do the report at all.

6. You have been saving your allowance for a new bike tire. Your friend wants you to go to a movie with him/her.
   a) You spend some money and go.
   b) You don't go.
   c) You ask your parents to give you money to spend at the movies.

Date_____

Today we did an activity called "Red Light, Green Light." The goal of this activity is to help students make wise choices about their behavior. Students were presented with some common choices for students their age. They then selected possible choices by standing in a part of the room that represented the choice with which they felt most comfortable. Students who were uncertain, chose to go stand in the center of the room at the red light. This allowed them an opportunity to "stop" and ponder the decision. We discussed some questions they could ask themselves when uncertain. These included: What do I want to happen? What is most important to me? What might the consequences of each decision be?

Sometimes students need to realize they may take their time to make wise decisions. Stopping to think teaches/students; to keep their focus on their goal, realize there may be more choices than they originally thought, and encourages them to ponder the possible consequences of their decision.

As a parent it can be difficult to watch your child make certain decisions. You can remind your child to stop and think. Discuss some of the decisions your child is facing and have him/her think through the consequences. Review the questions used in "Red Light, Green Light" to make decisions.

Sincerely,

_____

Water Babies

Objectives

Students will:

✔ discuss characteristics which represent responsible behavior

✔ list needs of a water baby

✔ brainstorm care taking behaviors that will meet the needs of the water baby.

✔ model appropriate nurturing behavior

Materials Needed

One water-filled balloon
"Adoption Certificate" handout
Index cards and pens

Procedures

1. Divide class into small groups.

2. Present to students a water filled balloon who is in need of nurturing.

3. Explain to students that a caretaking plan for the infant needs to be developed.

4. Each group will select a name for the baby.

5. Have groups of students brainstorm list of infant's needs.

6. Students will establish, in their small groups, a plan for meeting infants needs.

7. Group leaders will present groups' nurturing plan to remainder of the class.

8. Students will vote by confidential ballot (on index cards) on the caretaking plan that is the most responsible. The water baby will be given the name chosen by the group who wrote the most responsible care taking plan.

9. Tally the votes.

10. Present a certificate of adoption and a water baby to infant's new caretakers.

Discussion Questions

1. What behaviors in your family are signs of responsible behavior?
2. What behaviors do you display that are examples of being responsible?
3. Which step in the plan's development was the most difficult to generate?
4. When may it be necessary to ask for assistance in implementing your plan?
5. What resources are available to you if problems develop?
6. What problem-solving methods did you use when disagreements and conflicts concerning the plan occurred?
7. What did you learn from developing a caretaking plan that you may not have previously realized?

Variations

- Bags of sugar may be used in place of water balloons.
- Classroom pet such as a hedgehog may be used to take care of for a week.
- With parental permission, students may take turns taking home the class pet.
- Ask the first group to implement their plan for a week, and have them keep a log of problems and solutions they devised. At the end of the week, the first group becomes mentors to the second group. Have the second group implement their plan, keeping a log and revising their plan as needed. Continue the process allowing previous groups to become mentors to new groups until all groups have had an opportunity to be caregivers.
- Students may present caretaking skills at a career day presentation from the perspective of a caretaking cluster. The presentation may be given to younger students.
- Students could be trained as peer listners or mentors and paired up with a younger child who is experiencing some difficulty.

Adoption Certificate

This certifies that

_____

_____

was adopted on _____

at _____

Date_____

Today your child participated in the "Water Baby" activity which included teaching students how to recognize characteristics of responsible behavior, developing a list of infant's needs, and devising a plan for meeting those needs. Students evaluated each other's plans for responsible behavior.

It is never too early to begin to learn responsibility. Along with responsibility comes freedom.

Through the years you've taught your child responsibility and given them the space to use it. Discuss the ways the family and your individual child each show responsibility. As a parent, you may wish to have your child develop a responsible care taking plan for a pet or younger sibling. If feasible, allow the child to implement his/her plan. Follow implementation with a discussion about revisions for the plan.

Sincerely,

_____

Emerging Emotions

<table>
<tr><td>

Objectives

Students will:

- ✔ become aware of different emotions experienced through life events
- ✔ learn how they themselves, as well as peers, express their emotions
- ✔ brainstorm ways on how to express difficult emotions

</td><td>

Materials Needed

3x5 index cards
Access to outdoors
Colored markers

</td></tr>
</table>

Procedures

1. Divide class into small groups of 6-8 students.

2. On separate 3x5 index cards, write feelings each student may experience in their lives. For example: use words such as angry, sad, afraid, disappointed, happy, and jealous. Make sure each word is written with a different color marker. Use as many cards and words as there are students in each group.

3. Give one feeling card to each member of the group.

4. After members read the word, have them go outside with their cards.

5. Each member must find an object outside in the environment (Example: leaf, rock, etc). Keeping in mind their feeling word, the object chosen must represent that feeling. This object must make the students remember some event that occurred in their lives that elicited that emotional response.

6. Students gather back into their small groups.

7. Each group member takes a turn and explains the event they remembered, and how that event made them feel.

8. Group members explains what body language they used to express that feeling .

Discussion Questions

1. How did you feel when you were asked to think about and remember your life event?
2. Did you notice any common body language used among your group members to certain events?
3. Did you notice a variety of common objects chosen that brought forth similar emotions?
4. Do different objects bring out similar emotions?
5. How did you feel as each group member discussed their event?
6. After listening to each group member, was one emotion particularly difficult to remember or express over any other emotion?
7. Is there any one emotion discussed today that you feel you need to learn ways to express it more effectively?
8. How could you help one of your group members learn to allow themselves to feel and express a certain emotion?

Variations

- Emerging Emotions can be varied in several ways. Students can be asked to bring in objects from home, instead of objects from outdoors. If this activity is done on a rainy day, children may be asked to remember a certain place that reminded them of that emotion.
- Students can also develop feeling words privately before finding objects and sharing the event with the group. The group can develop feeling words collectively.
- After discussing objects and the event which elicited the feeling on the card, students can be placed into pairs where they can share their experiences and act them out in skits for the group members. Group members can even guess as to which emotion they are trying to convey.
- Students can bring in puppets, or other objects from home to help with showing these emotions, or they can simply draw how they feel on paper.
- As an outside follow up assignment, students can be asked to develop or bring in a song which represents that emotion written on their card.
- Students can use different colors to describe different emotions. Using different color paints or markers, students can create an emotions collage.
- Using different types of music, have the students discuss the different emotions that each type of music brings out in them.

Date_____

Dear Parent/Guardian:

Today in class students participated in small groups in an activity called "Emerging Emotions." Students were given index cards with emotions written on them. They were asked to go outside and find an object that reminded them of an event that made them feel the emotion on their card. Students discussed these emotions and how they each expressed them in everyday life.

Being aware of what common emotions are expressed will lead to strong communication skills. A large part of communication is non-verbal cues.

The warmth of your home is one non-verbal way of expressing your emotions. To help your child understand other non-verbal messages, you may use this activity between siblings or individually with their child. Ask children to pick objects out of the house that will make them remember an event that brought forth a certain emotion. You may have each child discuss the body language related to each emotion expressed, and to note any similarities or differences. You may also choose more creative ways to discuss emotions by using other modems such as music, stuffed animals, pictures, etc.

Sincerely,

_____

Climbing the Mountain to Responsible Behavior

Objectives

Students will:

✔ apply responsible behavior in real life situations

✔ brainstorm trouble shooting techniques needed to successfully complete the process for attaining characteristics of responsible behavior

✔ discuss importance of decision making skills and students' reactions

Materials Needed

Picture of a mountain
One penny
Question cards
Scissors
Index Cards (without lines)

Procedures

Set Up: Pass out index cards and have the students draw mountain climbing tools on them. Examples would be rope, harness, belay device (used to attach to your partner), crampons (spikes for boots), climbing boots, ice axe, and backpack. Be sure to have no more than 7 different tools. Label these "Tool Cards."

1. Divide class into groups of 4 to 7 students.

2. Place a picture of a mountain onto the floor. (See example on page 30)

3. Explain that they will be using their skills to climb the mountain to responsible behavior. There are seven levels on the mountain.

4. A student from each group will toss a penny onto the mountain and will answer a question (from the question card) from the level on which the penny lands. A group leader may be chosen who answers the question, or students may take turns within the groups.

5. If the student answers the question correctly, his/her team will receive a "Tool Card" for that level. If a team answers incorrectly, proceed to the next group.

6. The next group proceeds by repeating steps 4 and 5.

7. Each group continues taking turns, flipping pennies, and answering questions at the level they land on until one team has answered one question from the 7 levels and acquired all 7 different mountain climbing "Tool Cards."

8. The winning team then explains and discusses with the class the steps they learned that were needed to acquire characteristics that represent responsible behavior.

Discussion Questions

1. How did you feel as you were climbing your way up the mountain?
2. Did you find any particular level difficult to overcome?
3. Did you discover any one tool as being the most important over the other tools when climbing? If so, explain why.
4. What can happen if one tool is left out of the climbing process? How does this apply when making decisions in everyday life?
5. When climbing levels, did you find it more stressful to make decisions when deciding by yourselves, or were decisions harder to make when climbing as a team?
6. Give an example of a situation in your life where you can now apply these decision making skills more effectively than before you learned this lesson.
7. What future situations do you predict may occur that will force you to use effective decision making skills as well as displaying responsible behavioral reactions?
8. How can you continue to revise and improve your decision making skills?

Variations

- Instead of having a picture of a mountain and climbing those levels, students may be taken to an actual climbing wall center where they can climb those levels. The first team who climbs to the top of the climbing wall wins.
- Step Reeboks® may also be used as a way to represent levels to step up to in reaching the peak toward responsible behavior. Steps may be placed around the classroom with the appropriate amount of risers underneath that would represent levels reached toward responsible behavior. Team members would stand on the steps, answer those level questions, until one team has all its members on each riser.
- Instead of a picture of a mountain on the blackboard, a (large)mountain made out of construction paper may be taped onto the floor. Students could then toss beanbags onto the mountain levels and answer questions.
- Cards and pictures can be tailored to any other particular symbol besides a mountain. An example could be tools needed for firemen to rescue victims from a burning building.

Climbing the Mountain to Responsible Behavior

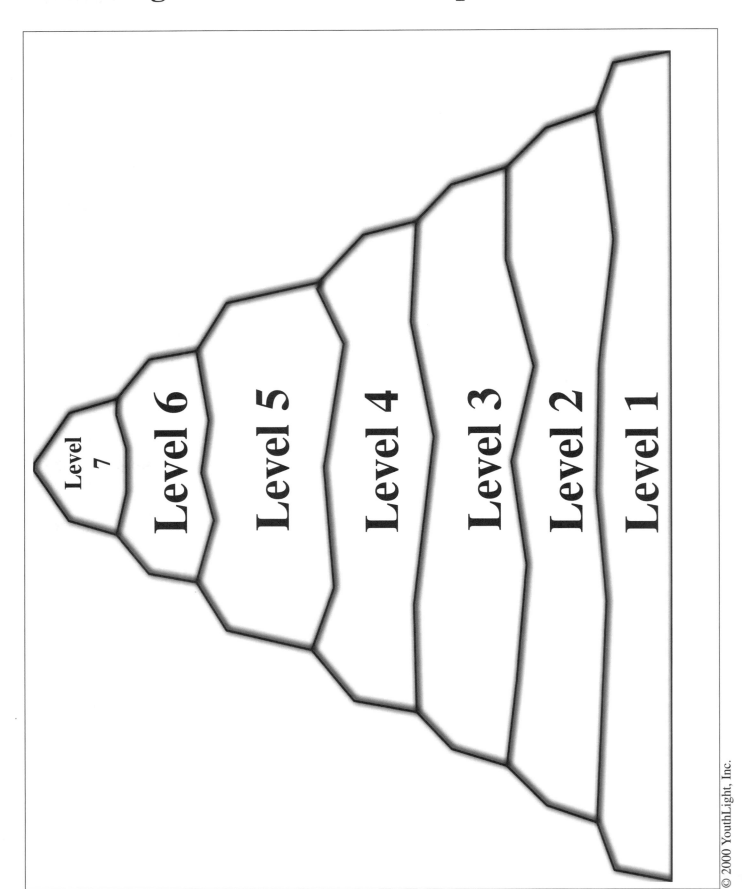

Climbing the Mountain to Responsible Behavior Questions

Cut on the dotted line.

#1 Level 1-Positive Pals

An example of how you cooperate with your partner is:

a. each partner explains conflict and acts out its consequences.
b. do not participate in role play at all.
c. hitting your partner because he/she has poor acting skills.

#2 Level 1-Positive Pals

The reason you weren't paired with your friends was:

a. to give you an opportunity to sit somewhere else.
b. to meet other kids in class.
c. because you have no friends.

#3 Level 1-Positive Pals

A student runs into you in the hallway and your books fall everywhere. An appropriate verbal response would be:

a. "It's okay, I know you didn't do it on purpose."
b. no verbal response, you just pick up your books and keep going, not mentioning how angry you are.
c. "Watch where you're going, you moron."

#4 Level 1-Positive Pals

Which of the student's thoughts reflect a positive self-image after receiving a poor test grade?

a. I didn't really study much anyway.
b. I'll ask the teacher for extra help so I can do better next time.
c. I'm so stupid, I can never get this right.

#5
Level 2-Cartoon Behaviors
True or False

T - F It is possible to have more than one feeling about a given event.

#6
Level 2-Cartoon Behaviors
True or False

T - F If you tell yourself you are capable you will feel successful.

Climbing the Mountain to Responsible Behavior Questions

Cut on the dotted line.

#7
Level 2-Cartoon Behaviors
True or False

T - F We can control our reactions.

#10 Level 3-Dear Diary

Who is responsible for recording the behavior?

a. The Teacher
b. The Student
c. Your pet iguana

#8
Level 2-Cartoon Behaviors
True or False

T - F Our thoughts cause our feelings.

#11 Level 3-Dear Diary

Which of the following could be an example of a recorded inappropriate behavior?

a. Swearing at the teacher.
b. Taking your time on a test.
c. Breathing.

#9 Level 3-Dear Diary

An example of how to record our behavior would be:

a. determine if the behavior is positive or negative, choose the corresponding notebook & sheet with your name on it, then write the behavior
b. React without thought.
c. It's never necessary to record behaviors. What's the point?

#12 Level 3-Dear Diary

Which of the following could be an example of a recorded appropriate behavior?

a. Getting to class on time.
b. Over sleeping and missing your first class.
c. Speaking without raising your hand.

Climbing the Mountain to Responsible Behavior Questions

Cut on the dotted line.

- -

#13 Level 4
Decision Making for All
True or False

T - F We can always improve our decision making skills

#16 Level 4
Decision Making for All
True or False

T - F Everyone knows the decision making process.

- -

#14 Level 4
Decision Making for All
True or False

T - F Decision making is a skill you need for life.

#17 Level 5-Red Light, Green Light
Someone who you do not find interesting asks you to a dance. Which of the following choices is the most appropriate?

a. Tell the person, "I'll get back to you."
b. Be honest and communicate how you feel.
c. Say "What's that smell?"

- -

#15 Level 4
Decision Making for All
True or False

T - F There are no right or wrong decisions.

#18 Level 5-Red Light, Green Light
Which of the following may be a way that your body tells you to take more time before making a decision?

a. You're bored and don't feel like thinking about it.
b. There is a nervous feeling in your stomach.
c. You have a heart attack.

- -

Climbing the Mountain to Responsible Behavior Questions

Cut on the dotted line.

#19 Level 5
Red Light, Green Light

When do people need to choose a "red" light?

a. When they feel stressed.
b. When your friends have chosen a red light.
c. Always - red is your favorite color.

#20 Level 5
Red Light, Green Light

Which of the following may be helpful to ask yourself when you're at a red light?

a. What should I do?
b. What will be the consequences of my actions.
c. Is it cool to be here?

#21 Level 6
Water Babies
True or False

T - F It is not necessary to meet all the needs of the water baby.

#22 Level 6
Water Babies
True or False

T - F Everyone is born knowing responsible behaviors.

#23 Level 6
Water Babies
True or False

T - F Care taking plans may be updated for efficiency.

#24 Level 6
Water Babies
True or False

T - F If one has care taking skills he/she will never encounter conflicts.

Climbing the Mountain to Responsible Behavior Questions

Cut on the dotted line.

#25 Level 7
Emerging Emotions
True or False

T - F An object can represent more than one emotion.

#26 Level 7
Emerging Emotions
True or False

T - F Through role plays, acceptable ways of expressing emotions can be learned.

#27 Level 7
Emerging Emotions
True or False

T - F Body language does not reflect a persons' emotions.

#28 Level 7
Emerging Emotions
True or False

Which of the following is a way to express anger in an acceptable manner?

a. Keep it inside and say nothing.
b. Talk about your anger.
c. Bang your head against the floor while screaming, "I'm so stupid!"

Climbing the Mountain to Responsible Behavior Answer Key

1.	a	15.	T
2.	b	16.	F
3.	a	17.	b
4.	b	18.	b
5.	T	19.	a
6.	T	20.	b
7.	T	21.	F
8.	T	22.	F
9.	a	23.	T
10.	b	24.	F
11.	a	25.	b
12.	a	26.	T
13.	T	27.	T
14.	T	28.	F

Date_____

Dear Parent/Guardian:

Today students reviewed the skills necessary for acquiring characteristics toward effective decision making as well as learning responsible behavior. Students played the game called "Climbing the Mountain to Responsible Behavior." Students flipped pennies, landed on mountain levels, answered questions pertaining to those levels until the skills and tools were acquired for reaching the peak of the mountain. The class discussed the reasons, reactions, and steps for learning responsible behavior and decision making.

At home you may use the same mountain technique but instead formulate your own event or conflict and allow your child to come up with the steps toward making an effective decision. You may have your child come up with ways to conquer each step on a weekly basis in order to allow your child time to develop effective decision making skills. You may also develop your own reward system at home when your child achieves each level.

Sincerely,

_____

Chapter 2

Tobacco, Alcohol and Other Drugs

"Good and evil, reward and punishment, are the only motives to a rational creature: these are the spur and reins whereby all mankind are set on work, and guided."

- John Locke

The goal of the tobacco, alcohol and other drugs chapter is to help students take responsibility for their decisions and to realize that their actions have consequences. Prevention and awareness are stressed. Lessons include defining drugs, identifying thoughts and feelings which may be associated with their use, peer pressure, saying no, identifying stress, using relaxation activities, analyzing family roles, and listing alternatives to using tobacco, alcohol and other drugs.

What's the Deal on Drugs?

Objectives

Students will:
- ✔ define "drugs."
- ✔ teach students to determine if a substance is a drug or not.

Materials Needed

Pencil
Paper
"Drug Fact" handout
Craft supplies (for students to make game)

Procedures

1. Make sure students have pencil and paper. Ask students to write everything they know about drugs and give them time to write.

2. Discuss what they know or think is true about drugs.

3. Give the students the "Drug Fact" handout and discuss.

4. Have the students list examples of substances that are not drugs.

5. In small groups, have students develop games to teach younger students about examples of drugs and other substances that are not drugs. Examples of games may include: drug bingo, memory card game.

6. Play games and revise.

Discussion Questions

1. If you had information about drugs prior to this activity, where did you get your information?
2. As a participant, from which game did you learn the most?
3. Did you learn more from making a game or playing a game?
4. What do you feel would be the worst effect or cost for using drugs?
5. Is there ever any harm in taking a prescription drug? If so, when can it be harmful?
6. Have you ever been adversely effected by drugs?
7. On a scale of one to ten, (1=not that important and 10=very important) how important is it to remain drug free?

Variations

- Instead of using games, students may write songs or perform skits to teach the information to younger students.
- Initial description of current information students have on drugs may be done with a partner.
- The fact sheet may be developed into a quiz and/or a pre or post test.
- A video explaining drugs may be used in place of the discussion.
- Volunteers such as DARE officers or nurses may be used in the discussion.
- As an additional activity, drug dogs may be presented by the police.
- Students can create a skit about drugs showing their negative affects. They may perform their skits in class and for the school.

What's the Deal on Drugs?
Drug Fact Handout

Definition: A drug is any substance put in or on the body, other than food, that brings about a physical or emotional change.

Categories:

Depressants   Slows down voluntary and involuntary responses.
Examples: Heroin, Opium, Codeine, Morphine, liquor, wine, beer, Valium, Librium, gasoline

Stimulants   Speed up the voluntary and involuntary responses.
Examples: tobacco, Ritalin, coffee, soft drinks, diet pills, Cocaine and speed

Hallucinogens   Alter perceptions and cause hallucinations
Examples: Marijuana, Hashish, LSD, PCP

Uses for Drugs :

Prevent diseases   Examples: vaccines, antibiotics, vitamins

Fighting diseases   Examples: aspirin, antibiotics, chemotherapy

Maintain our health   Examples: Insulin, antihistamines, Dilantin (epilepsy), vitamins, Lithium

Change our moods   Examples: alcohol, marijuana, coffee, nicotine, LSD

Possession or use of some of these drugs is illegal.

How to know if you're taking a prescription drug safely

1. Only take a prescription that was prescribed for you.
2. Do not take more than the dosage indicated by the doctor (on the bottle).
3. Do not take any other drugs in combination with the prescription without your doctor's consent.
4. Follow directions completely, for example:

    ☞Take with food and water

    ☞If indicated on bottle, take full amount of the dosage

    ☞Take at the time of day instructed

Date_____

Dear Parent/Guardian:

Today students learned facts about drugs in the activity "What's the Deal on Drugs?" Students developed games and taught youngsters to identify examples of drugs and other substances that are not drugs.

As a parent you are constantly faced with the reality of the existence of drugs in our schools. Continue to keep communication open between you and your child as he/she may be confronted with situations involving drugs. Helping your child learn the facts about drugs will help them make wise choices in and out of school.

To review, you may want to ask your child to tell you about drugs. To further get to know your child, ask him/her what first hand knowledge he/she has of drugs and how he/she obtained this information. Ask you child how he/she feels about drugs. You may share with your child your views of drugs.

Sincerely,

_____

Name That Tune

Objectives

Students will:

✔ listen to music by artists who died from drug use

✔ identify the artist who performed the music

✔ discuss feelings expressed in the music and thoughts that surfaced while listening to the music

Materials Needed

Paper

Pen or pencil

Recorded music
(by artists who died from drug use)

CD/Cassette player

Procedures

Set Up: (To be assigned at least one night prior to activity)

From their personal collections, have students bring in music written or performed by artists who have died from drugs, tobacco, or alcohol abuse.

1. Ask students to identify the artist who has died from drug, tobacco, or alcohol abuse.

2. Choose a student to play a song that he/she has brought to the group.

3. Ask students to identify the title and artist for each song. If they do not recognize the song or artist, as a group give the answer.

4. Discuss emotions expressed in the music.

5. Distribute paper and pens to students.

6. Ask students to draw facial expressions to show a possible emotion expressed by the music.

7. Below the facial expression, have students write the thoughts they had while hearing the music.

8. Discuss the students' feelings and thoughts while listening to the music.

9. Discuss the possible relationship between these feelings and drug use or addiction.

10. Repeat steps 2 through 9 with other songs.

Discussion Questions

1. What led you to identify and associate the emotion you chose with each song?
2. Was there an instance when you felt an emotion identified in a song? How did you deal with that emotion?
3. Did others identify different emotions with the same song? If yes, why? If no, could there be other emotions?
4. Did the emotion you associated with any song change throughout the song? If so, at what point in the music and why?
5. Choose one of the emotions discussed. How can drug use effect how someone might deal with that emotion?
6. How can music be used to communicate an emotion? What other methods may be used to communicate emotions?
7. If the feelings you felt while listening to the music upset you, what did or could you do about that?

Variations

- Put students in groups, see which group generates the most artists who have died as a result of drug use.
- Students will take a song or a portion of a song and use drama or puppets to display the emotion(s) being expressed.
- Use a variety of instruments to perform songs for students. It may be arranged ahead of time for students to perform songs for their peers.
- Students may sculpt facial features into clay heads expressing emotions expressed in the songs.
- In teams, have kids develop a rap, country, reggae, etc. song to express the emotion they identified in a song played during the activity.

Date_____

Dear Parent/Guardian:

In today's activity, "Name That Tune", we listened to music by artists who died as an effect of drug use. Students then identified the artists who performed the music. We discussed the feelings and thoughts students had while listening to the music. Students identified the connection between thoughts and feelings. Students expressed possible feelings associated with drug use or addiction.

Discuss with your child the possible emotional affects of music. It's important to be aware of how music affects your child's perception of him/herself and the world around him/her. Ask your child what music he/she likes to listen to, how it makes him/her feel, and what things he/she does while listening to the music. Share with your child your own responses to those questions.

Sincerely,

_____

Family Feud

This activity will require more than one sessions to complete

Objectives

Students will:

✔ communicate personal and family values, drug facts, alternate activities to do instead of using drugs

✔ earn points to identify the major ideas under categories discussed with family

Materials Needed

Pencil

Paper

"Family Portrait" handout

"Family Activities" handout

"Family Drug Information" handout

Procedures

Set Up: (To be assigned at least one night prior to activity)

Pass out "Family Portrait", "Family Activities" and "Family Drug Information" handouts. Read the directions and answer the questions. Inform the students to take these handouts home, complete and return.

Gather complete materials from students and tally results given for each handout separately. For example: On the "Family Portrait" handouts, list each different value given on the handouts. Then beside each value put a tally mark each time that value appears on any other student's handout. Follow the same procedure for all 3 handouts. List the top 4 answers for each handout.

1. Put the students into groups of 3. Have each group choose a team leader. Tell the students that the objective for each group is to earn as many points as possible.

2. For 30 seconds, the group leaders will ask the group members what top 4 values appeared on the "Family Portrait" handouts.

3. The group leaders will write the responses on paper.

4. The group leaders will share the responses with the class.

5. Reveal to the class the top 4 values that were found when the class results were tallied.

6. Assign one point for each group answer that matches the class results.

7. Allow groups to choose a new leader and repeat the steps above for the "Family Activities" and "Family Drug Information" handouts.

8. Tally the total group points. The group with the most points is the winner.

Discussion Questions

1. Which family members participated in your discussion?
2. What role did you play in the discussion itself?
3. How do you feel about the discussion and your role in it?
4. Is this a typical family discussion? If so, how is it typical?
5. If you could change one thing about your family discussion, what would you change?

Variations

- If a child feels his/her family does not have discussions, have him/her make up a scene about a topic he/she would like to discuss with his/her family.
- Students may act out discussions.
- Students may illustrate discussions using cartoon bubbles to indicate what is said.

Family Feud
Family Portrait Handout

Family Feud
Family Activities Handout

With your family list the activities you would participate in instead of doing drugs.

1. _____

2. _____

3. _____

4. _____

5. _____

6. _____

7. _____

8. _____

Family Feud
Family Drug Information Handout

With your family discuss and list facts concerning drugs.

1. _____

2. _____

3. _____

4. _____

5. _____

6. _____

7. _____

8. _____

9. _____

10. _____

Date_____

Dear Parent/Guardian:

The "Family Feud" activity was designed to generate a family discussion on drug information and family values.

Now that your child has had an opportunity to discuss with you as a family and classmates values regarding drug use, you may wish to discuss how your child will apply this information to real life events. Ask your child what situations he/she has experienced concerning drug use and how he/she dealt with those experiences. If the experiences have been limited, you may wish to generate scenarios and discuss possible ideas incorporating family values.

Sincerely,

_____

Pressure Cooker

Objectives

Students will:

✔ experience peer pressure in a game

✔ define peer pressure

Materials Needed

Pen or pencil
Paper
"Task List" handout

Procedures

1. Explain to the students that they will play the game "Pressure Cooker." The objective of the game is for each group to work to earn the most points. Points are earned when the students succeed in persuading their partners to complete "tasks" with various point values.

2. Divide the class into 3 groups. Choose one group to be "Group A", another "Group B", and the third "Group C." "Group A" will start first.

3. Pair the students in "Group A" and instruct them to choose who will be the "Persuader" and who will be the "Performer." Assign to each pair a neutral student from another group to keep score for the pair. Instruct the students that they may not open the sealed task list until they are told to do so. Warn students that at no time are they permitted to tell the point value for any task listed. Explain to the "Scorekeepers" that they are to mark on their list of tasks the ones the performers complete in the given amount of time. The "Persuaders" have the option of presenting tasks in any order they desire. Inform the "Performers" that they have the option of passing or completing the tasks that are presented. Tell the "Persuaders" and "Performers" that they will have five minutes to earn as many points as possible by performing tasks.

4. Give the "Persuaders" and the "Scorekeepers" a sealed copy of the tasks with an assigned point value. Tell them to open the sealed copy and begin persuading. Immediately begin keeping time for five minutes.

5. At the end of the five minutes, tell the group to stop.

6. Have each "Scorekeeper" total the points.

7. List the points earned by each pair on paper or the chalkboard and then add to get a total point value for the group.

8. Repeat steps 3,4,5,6,and 7 for "Group B" and "Group C."

9. Allow the students to give their definitions of peer pressure.

10. Define peer pressure.

Discussion Questions

1. What did the "Persuader" do if you passed on a task and how did you feel?
2. Did any performers change his/her mind about doing a task when he/she heard the "Persuader?"
3. As an observer, which role did you perceive as being more pressure filled?
4. What could you do if this were a real life situation and your friends are encouraging you to do something you are not sure you want to do?
5. How do your bodies feel when you do not want to do something and others are trying to convince you?
6. Have you ever felt peer pressure?

Variations

- Play "Pressure Cooker" first without allowing teammate encouragement, then allow it.
- Have the students generate the list of tasks to be completed.
- Have the students generate a list of pressure-filled situations. Two students will then "pressure" the student who generated the ideas into agreeing to do at least one of the ideas.

Pressure Cooker
"Task List" Handout

Group A

(5 points)	Hop around the room like a frog, while barking like a dog.
(5 points)	Do "The Bunny Hop."
(10 points)	Sing "Twinkle, Twinkle Little Star."
(15 points)	Tell what characteristics you find attractive in a person?
(5 points)	Name a momento or souvenir that you have kept, which no one knows about.
(10 points)	When you are angry at your parents, what things do you do to anger or embarrass them?

Group B

(10 points)	Skip around the room and sing "Yankee Doodle."
(15 points)	Do "Ring Around the Rosie" with me.
(5 points)	In front of the whole class, tell someone in this room something possitive about him/her.
(10 points)	Which teacher do you dislike the most?
(5 points)	When was the last time you cried and why?
(5 points)	What quality about yourself would you most like to change?

Group C

(15 points)	Do the "Hokie Pokie" dance.
(5 points)	Find someone in the audience to strut around the room flapping their wings and clucking like a chicken with you.
(10 points)	Tell your most embarrassing moment.
(5 points)	Have you ever lied? Give an example.
(5 points)	When was the last time your were scared and why?
(10 points)	What would it take for you to trust someone?

Date_____

Dear Parent/Guardian:

In a safe environment, the students had an opportunity to experience peer pressure through participation in the game "Pressure Cooker." By playing "Pressure Cooker" and discussing it, the students were able to identify peer pressure and react to it.

Awareness of peer pressure is necessary in remaining loyal to one's own values. As a parent, you have worked to establish values in your child for many years. Discuss with your child when he/she has felt peer pressure and from whom the pressure came. Continue to keep the lines of communication open with your child regarding peer pressure, drugs, alcohol, tobacco and other issues your child may face in the future.

Sincerely,

_____

The Pressure's On

Objectives

Students will:

✔ list ways to say "no."

✔ dramatize saying "no" to person(s) offering drugs.

✔ rank social situations involving peer pressure according to the difficulty involved in saying "no."

Materials Needed

Pen or pencil
Paper
"Peer Pressure Situation" handout

Procedures

1. Discuss various ways of saying no. (Say no, say no repeatedly, name consequences, suggest alternate activities, walk away)

2. As a whole group, create scenarios where drugs are being offered.

3. Divide class into groups and assign each group a scenario to dramatize for peers. Encourage each group to use more than one way of saying no.

4. Allow students to perform scenarios for peers.

5. Discuss effectiveness of methods chosen to say no.

6. Pass out "Peer Pressure Situation" handout.

7. Individually, have students rank the situations according to difficulty in saying no.
   1 - most difficult situation in which to say no
   10 - easiest situation in which to say no

8. Discuss difficulty level of situations and what made situations difficult or easy.

Discussion Questions

1. Have you ever faced a situation in which it was difficult to say no? What ways did you try?
2. What other ways are there to say no?
3. Have you ever been in a situation where you chose to say no and how did it feel?
4. Is there ever a cost for saying no? If so, what? Is the cost worth it?
5. How assertive do you have to be to say no?

Variations

- To save time, scenarios could be prepared in advance. Prepared scenarios can be chosen out of a hat and students say no, with no advance preparation.
- Older students could be brought in to dramatize actual life situations to which they have said no.
- Instead of ranking by numbers, students could cut apart situations and put most difficult at top of the desk to least difficult at the bottom of desk.

The Pressure's On
"Peer Pressure Situation" Handout

_____ 1. A friend asks you to come over to his/her house to drink beer. His/her parents won't be home.

_____ 2. A friend has keys to his/her parents' car, but is not old enough to drive. He/she wants you to go for a ride with him/her.

_____ 3. A couple of your friends approach you in the hallway and ask you to go to their house to watch an adult video.

_____ 4. A group of your classmates tells you if you take a copy of the test answers from the teacher's desk, they will be friends with you.

_____ 5. An older group of students are smoking a joint and offer you a hit.

_____ 6. A group of new friends invite you to skip school to go skinny dipping at a near by lake.

_____ 7. A friend takes his older brother's cigarettes and wants you to smoke them with him.

_____ 8. At a party, kids are pairing off and going to secluded areas. You are being pressured to participate.

_____ 9. You approach a music store and see a CD you want in the window, your friends suggest you go in and take it when the clerk is not looking.

_____ 10. A student who has repeatedly called you and your friends names walks by and knocks your books out of your hands. Your friends tell you to punch him/her.

Date_____

Dear Parent/Guardian:

The lesson, "The Pressure's On" gave students an opportunity to practice saying no to peer pressure in realistic situations. The students ranked social situations according to the difficulty involved in saying no. The reason for the difficulty in saying no was discussed.

Everyone will face peer pressure at some point in time. Knowing one's self well and being prepared to combat unwanted pressure, will ease the situation. You may wish to explore further the actual peer pressure with which your child has been faced. Older siblings can contribute ones they, too, have faced. You may want to discuss family values, ways of saying no, personal values and responsibility with your child. Continuing to be a strong role model and letting your child know how you feel about drugs will give them the strength they need to conquer unwelcomed events.

Sincerely,

_____

Breaking Free From Drugs

Objective

Students will:

✔ think of creative and healthy ways the layers of stress can be removed.

Materials Needed

Bulletin board
Paper
Tape
Story or video on alcohol or drugs and how it's affecting students' lives

Procedures

1. Have students brainstorm a list of ways drugs and alcohol affect individuals in families.

2. Show a video or read a story that relates to this discussion.

3. Randomly select a student to play the role of the person affected by the drugs and alcohol in the video or story.

4. Allow students to make a list of the various ways the person's life was affected by the alcohol and drug use.

5. Read one item from the list and choose two students to wrap and tape a piece of bulletin board paper around the affected person's arms and midriff.

6. Continue reading one item at a time. Choose new students and add a layer until all items have been read.

7. Have students come up with healthy ways to remove the layers of stress caused by the drug and alcohol use.

8. Read one item from the list, choosing a student to remove the outer layer of paper.

9. Continue reading items while choosing different students to remove the outer layer until only one layer remains.

10. Read the last item on the list and have the affected individual break through the last layer of paper.

Discussion Questions

1. How do you think it would feel to be the individual who was covered by the layers of stress?
2. Was it easier to come up with ways others could help the person, or ways the person could help him/herself?
3. How do you think it would feel to finally break through the layers?
4. Once broken through the layers, is the problem solved for good?
5. Do you see any layers that are similar to ones in your life?
6. What methods have you used in the past to break through layers? Which of those were effective?

Variations

- Have one student remove all the layers from the affected individual.
- Use jackets, shirts, or blankets in place of the paper to represent the layers.
- Have the students write a story to be presented to the class showing the layers of damage in an individual's life.
- Divide a larger group into smaller groups and allow each group to put on and take off layers.
- Write stressful events on the layers of paper as they are taped to the person.

Date_____

Dear Parent/Guardian:

In today's lesson, "Breaking Free from Drugs", we talked about the unhealthy layers of stress which accumulate through the use of drugs or alcohol. We also looked at ways to remove those layers and reduce stress. We discussed how those layers felt and affected lives.

No one is completely free of layers, even if drugs and alcohol have not played a part in forming those layers. The intensity of the layers may be deceptive. The removal of the layers will take work but will result in a greater self-awareness, reduced stress and increased self-esteem.

Discuss with your child the layers in his/her life. These layers may be unresolved issues or problems. Examine the methods your child has used to try to solve the problem. You can be instrumental in trying to come up with ways to remove these stressful layers or to prevent future layers from forming. Removal of the layers will require your T.L.C. as it is a sensitive time.

Sincerely,

_____

Hodge Podge

Objectives

Students will:

✔ develop a list of activities that can be done in place of using drugs.

✔ share activities with peers.

Materials Needed

Magazines
Newspapers
Clay
Yarn
Poster board
Markers
Paint
Material scraps

Procedures

1. Have the students lists things they like to do, as well as things others may enjoy.

2. Brainstorm creative methods to communicate ideas about their interest to others (examples: collage of pictures representing activities, painting depicting ideas, poems).

3. Explain to students where materials are located and allow them to gather as needed.

4. Students will work individually on a display that represents their list of ideas.

5. Take turns sharing these ideas with others.

6. As individuals share ideas, generate a group list of activities including all these ideas.

Discussion Questions

1. What activities were mentioned by your peers that you could do but haven't done before?

2. Were any activities listed in which you no longer participate? If so, why do you no longer do them?

3. Which display most effectively communicated ideas for activities?

4. How could using drugs effect the activities and your performance in them?

5. What effect have drugs played on the activities of those close to you?
6. How can participating in enjoyable activities effect your decision concerning drug use?

Variations

- Allow students to work in teams. Have the students divide into groups and see which group can generate the greatest number of activities. Give an award to the student who has participated in the most activities from the class list of ideas.

- Have students use a variety of creative methods such as developing skits or writing a song to communicate ideas. Ask students the day before the activity to bring in materials from home or from outside to use for the displays.

- Allow students class time to participate in new activities from the class list.

- Bring in outside volunteers to lead students in these activities.

Date_____

Dear Parent/Guardian:

Today was a "Hodge Podge" of ideas. Students brainstormed a list of activities in which they could participate, instead of using drugs. We then employed creative techniques in which to communicate these ideas with one another. The students shared their ideas with their peers.

Students who are actively involved and have interests they pursue will feel connected, have a higher self-esteem, and will have a greater opportunity to meet others with similar interests.

No one knows your child better than you do. You can begin to help your child get to know him/herself. At home, you may choose to discuss enjoyable family activities that can be done instead of using drugs. This may be an opportunity to discuss your family views on drug use. As a result, a family activity night may be developed.

Sincerely,

_____

Drug Wrap

<table>
<tr><td>

Objective

Students will:

✔ apply knowledge gained in Tobacco, Alcohol, and Other Drugs chapter

</td><td>

Materials Needed

Octahedron
"Drug Wrap Questions"
Clock or timer

</td></tr>
</table>

Procedures

Set Up: Copy Octahedron handout, cut out, and assemble.

1. Divide group into teams of four members.

2. Prior to starting the game set a time limit and make sure all participants are aware of the limit.

3. Explain the rules of the game to students as follows. The objective is to score more points than any other team. Points are scored by correctly answering questions.

4. Randomly choose a team to go first.

5. One person from this team rolls the octahedron.

6. This person must answer a question. Read a question from the lesson corresponding to the lesson name on the side of the octahedron that is on top. The person who rolled the octahedron has thirty seconds to answer the question. If the person answers correctly, his/her team is awarded a point.

7. Rotate around the room to each team.

8. Have a different team member answer each question.

Discussion Questions

1. What have you learned after participating in the lessons about drugs?
2. How will you apply this to your everyday life?
3. Who do drugs effect and how may it effect them?
4. Where could you get additional information about drugs?
5. What questions do you currently have about drugs?
6. Can peer pressure be escaped?

Variations

- Instead of setting a time limit a limit of points may be used.
- You may choose to use lesson numbers, in place of the lesson name on the sides of the octahedron.
- Write each question on a separate index card. Students will randomly select a card and answer the question rather than roll the octahedron.
- You may elect to allow team members to give input before the participant answers the question.
- In addition to answering the question, students may be required to generate a story that represents the answer.
- Students may develop their own questions to use in the game.

Drug Wrap
Octahedron

To assemble the octahedron (eight-sided die):
Cut out as one solid piece.
Fold along each side of each triangle, so the words are exposed and on the outside.
Tape or glue the tabs that read "Fold and seal."

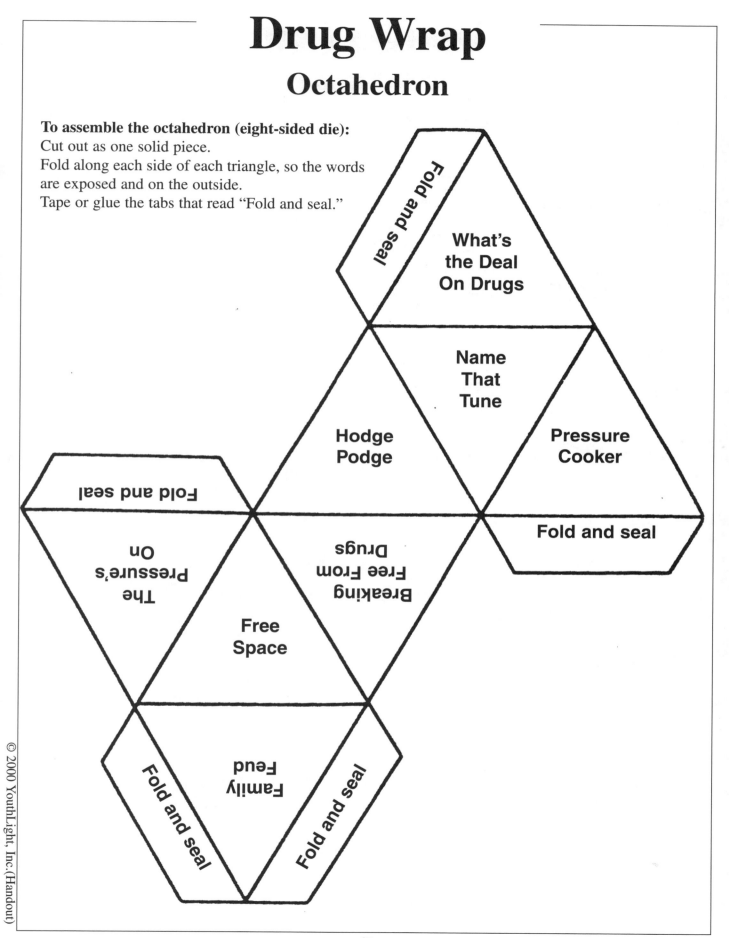

Fold and seal

What's the Deal On Drugs

Name That Tune

Hodge Podge

Pressure Cooker

Fold and seal

Fold and seal

The Pressure's On

Breaking Free From Drugs

Fold and seal

Free Space

Family Feud

Fold and seal

Fold and seal

Drug Wrap
Questions

The correct answers to the questions listed below are located at the end of the question in parentheses.

What's the Deal On Drugs

1. True or False   Chocolate contains a drug. (T)
2. True or False   Vitamins are drugs.(T)
3. True or False   Mood altering drugs include aspirin, Insulin, and vaccines. (3)
4. True or False   Possession of drugs is always illegal. (F)
5. True or False   If you are taking a prescription drug and it is not working, you should increase the dosage. (F)

Name That Tune

1. True or False   Music can be used to create an emotion. (T)
2. True or False   Upon hearing the same song, two persons can experience two different emotions. (T)
3. True or False   Drug use and drug addiction are the same thing. (F)
4. True or False   Drugs can affect your ability to recognize your feelings. (T)
5. True or False   Your thoughts and feelings can change throughout the same piece of music. (T)

Family Feud

1. True or False   Everyone in a family will have the same values. (F)
2. True or False   Throughout your life, your values will remain the same. (F)
3. True or False   Running is an alternate activity to doing drugs. (T)
4. True or False   Doing drugs is a choice. (T)
5. Give an activity you can do instead of doing drugs. (Accept any reasonable answer)

Pressure Cooker

1. True or False   Many people experience peer pressure. (T)
2. True or False   The result of peer pressure is always negative. (F)
3. True or False   Peer pressure is when all your friends tackle you, and as a group pin you to the ground. (F)
4. True or False   Peer pressure only happens to teens. (F)
5. True or False   Peer pressure can cause stress.(T)

Drug Wrap
Questions

The correct answers to the questions listed below are located at the end of the question in parentheses.

The Pressure's On

1. True or False   You feel more peer pressure in certain situations. (T)
2. True or False   It is better to be aggressive, rather than assertive, in dealing with peer pressure. (F)
3. True or False   There is only one way to say no to peer pressure. (F)
4. True or False   There may be a cost for saying no. (T)
5. True or False   By watching others deal with peer pressure, you may learn effective ways to deal with it yourself. (T)

Breaking Free From Drugs

1. True or False   There are many layers or ways drugs can effect people. (T)
2. True or False   Breaking through drugs means destroying the protective seal around a bottle of aspirin. (F)
3. True or False   Once a person breaks through the layers of drugs, he/she will never be affected by drugs again. (F)
4. True or False   The only person who is affected by drugs is the one who is taking them. (T)
5. True or False   There is always an easy way to break free from drugs. (F)

Hodge Podge

1. True or False   Having activities you enjoy is a good tool to use in avoiding drug use. (T)
2. True or False   The activities a person enjoys may change throughout his or her life. (T)
3. True or False   Substituting one drug for the use of another is an alternate activity to taking drugs. (F)
4. True or False   Swimming, biking, and talking to friends may be done instead of taking drugs. (T)
5. True or False   People who take drugs never have any hobbies. (F)

Date_____

Dear Parent/Guardian:

Today's game, "Drug Wrap", included a review of drugs, stress, peer pressure, and alternate activities to taking drugs. It also covered thoughts and feelings associated with drug use.

This would be a perfect time to talk with your child about drugs. Share with him/her your views about drug use. Ask your child to share with you situations he/she has faced concerning drugs.

The warmth, love, and belonging you provide for your child will encourage your child to choose options other than drug use.

Sincerely,

_____

Chapter 3

Grief, Loss and Transition

*"Emotion is the chief source of all becoming-conscious.
There can be no transforming of darkness into
light and of apathy into movement without emotion."*

- Carl Gustav Jung

The grief, loss and transition chapter gives students an opportunity to acknowledge their feelings of loss and to work through those feelings. The chapter is designed to increase awareness of the stages and to teach coping techniques. Students will define loss, examine emotional and behavioral reactions to loss, identify stages of loss, examine grief from a cultural perspective, and learn to say goodbye.

Sticky Situation

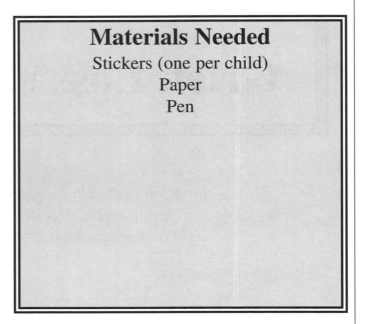

Objectives

Students will:
- ✔ define loss
- ✔ list examples of losses
- ✔ individually rank losses

Materials Needed

Stickers (one per child)
Paper
Pen

Procedures

1. Give each student a sticker

2. Randomly approach a few students and take away from the students the sticker.

3. Ask students what just happened.

4. Tell what a loss is by giving an example of it or by attaching an emotion to an experience.

5. Put students into pairs and have them generate a list of losses people experience.

6. As a whole group, make a master list containing all losses identified by pairs.

7. Have each student choose the ten losses that would be most difficult for him/her to experience. Students will rank these from 1 to 10, with 1 being least difficult and 10 being most difficult.

8. Allow students to share their lists and comment as to why they ranked the losses in that order.

9. Return the stickers to the students from whom you took them.

10. Ask what it felt like to get the sticker back. Define the transition.

11. Look at the list of losses again, and have students determine if they would move any of the listed items from the category of loss to the category of transition.

Discussion Questions

1. How would you describe your feelings when (or if) the sticker was removed?
2. How does loss affect a person's life?
3. How did you determine which loss would be the most difficult for you to face?
4. What examples of loss were mentioned that you had not considered a loss?
5. What could some of the long range effects of losses be?
6. What is the difference between a loss and a transition?
7. Did you disagree with whether an event was categorized as a loss or a transition?

Variations

- Candy may be used in place of stickers.
- Show a video or pictures of losses. Then students can list the losses seen.
- When students are ranking losses, they may vote as a whole class on most difficult loss.
- Begin the lesson with a pre-test which asks the students to define loss and what losses they have experienced.
- The day before doing this lesson, ask students to bring to school (with parent's permission) their favorite possession. Use this object to discuss what it would be like to lose something.

Date_____

Dear Parent/Guardian:

The overall goal of "Sticky Situation" was to differentiate between loss and transition and to experience both. Students defined loss and listed examples of various losses. They ranked the losses according to which ones would be most difficult for them to have to face. Students also defined, ranked and listed transitions.

All of us experience transitions and losses at certain times in our lives. People's perception of the same event may differ. With time, one's perspective of a particular event may change.

You have been there for your child through many transitions or losses. You may wish to provide your child with an opportunity to tell what transitions and losses he/she is currently experiencing, and how he/she feels about them. Remember, he/she may see things in a much different light than you do. It's important to listen to your child's views with an open mind. You may also want to discuss any transitions or losses that concern him/her. If there has been any traumatic loss(es) in your child's life you may want to inform the guidance counselor at your school.

Sincerely,

_____

Life Raft

Objective

Students will:

✔ examine different emotional and behavioral reactions to loss.

Materials Needed

Coins (see steps under procedure to determine necessary number of each)

Flat piece of Styrofoam or plastic to be used as "life raft"

Permanent marker

Container large enough in which Styrofoam or plastic container can float

Water

Procedures

Set up: (do before participants arrive)

    a. Gather "life raft", coins, and container.

    b. Fill the container three-fourths the way full of water.

    c. Float the "life raft" in the container of water

    d. Test to see how many coins it takes to sink the "life raft."

    e. Remove raft from water and dry.

    f. Using the permanent marker, put a line down the center of the raft.

    g. Prepare two piles of coins. Each pile should contain enough coins to sink the raft plus an additional few. Make sure each pile has an equal number of each denomination(s) of coins.

1. Randomly divide group into two teams.

2. Allow the students to choose names for the teams.

3. Explain:

Objective of game: Place coins on a raft without sinking it.

Procedure of game: A player from the first team claims a side of the raft for his/her team by placing a coin on that side. A player from the opposing team places a coin on the opposite side. Play continues in this fashion until the raft sinks.

4. Begin the game.

5. Have the "winning" team list the physical reactions expressed by the team that sunk the raft. At the same time, have the team that sunk the raft, list how they felt about the loss.

6. State what feelings you think the opposing team felt at the end of the game. What physical characteristics did they exhibit that led you to this conclusion?

Discussion Questions

1. How does this loss relate to possible losses in your life?
2. The team who sunk the raft experienced the same event, why were there different reactions from team members?
3. What were you feeling while placing a coin on the raft that was near sinking?
4. Did students who were experiencing the same emotion, behave the same or differently?
5. How did the "winning" team feel when they saw the reactions of the team that sunk the raft?

Variations

- To make the raft able to tip as opposed to sinking, put a thumb tack through the center of the raft and through the tip of a pencil, so the pencil is perpendicular to the raft. Construct a clay platform, on which a marble will rest, at the lead end of the pencil. Place a marble on the platform.

- Instead of allowing students to choose which coin they wish to use, make a spinner which list each option. To make a spinner, cut out a cardboard circle. Divide the circle into four equal quadrants. List one of each of the following in each quadrant: penny, nickel, dime, quarter. Cut a "pointer" out of the cardboard. Through the center of the pointer place a brass-plated fastener pointing downward. Push the pointed end of the fastener through the center point of the circle, so the pointer rests on top of the circle. Underneath the circle, bend the legs of the fastener, so the fastener is secured. Make certain the pointer will spin easily as it is tapped.

- Do the above activity by placing students in groups and allowing each group to play the game.

- Milk cartons from lunch may be washed and used. Each team may use their own carton. Use only one denomination of coins. Teams will take turns placing a coin in their carton, until a carton sinks.

Date_____

Dear Parent/Guardian:

Today the students played the "Life Raft" game. In this game, a team experienced losing. Students were asked to observe each other to identify physical characteristics of how their opponents may be feeling. The students were then asked how they thought about the loss.

Everyone experiences minor losses, such as not winning a game, recognizing how people may feel after such a loss allows us to understand others and ourselves better. Your child also had the opportunity to realize that not everybody will feel the same way given the same situation.

Discuss with your child the losses he/she has experienced. It's always difficult to see your child go through a loss but you can ease the transition by continuing to offer your support during this time. You may ask what emotions he/she remembers feeling and how he/she expressed those feelings. A further discussion may be done regarding the observations your child has had of others who have experienced a loss and what he/she recalls of that person's behavior concerning the loss.

Sincerely,

_____

Take Five

Objectives

Students will:
- ✔ state and define the stages of grief
- ✔ categorize the stages of grief

Materials Needed

Mask handout
"Five Stages of Grief"handout
Pen
Markers
Scissors
5 popsicle sticks
4 different colored balls

Procedures

1. Read and allow students time to comprehend the five stages of grief. Use the following activity to explain the person's movement through the stages of grief: Put the students in a circle. Give them four different colored balls. Have them pass each ball clockwise. While they are passing the balls, have one student outside the circle, facing away from the circle, count to five. When the student who is counting gets to five, write on the board who is holding a ball and what color they have. At the same time the balls are being passed and the student is counting to five, have another student stand outside the circle, facing away from the circle, randomly say "toss." Each time he/she says "toss" the person holding each ball will throw it to another person on the opposite side of the circle. Discuss how this activity relates to a person's movement through the stages of grief. Explain a person may move from one stage to another circularly (the passing of the ball form one person to another), but may also jump around periodically (tossing of the ball).

2. Students will make up questions and ask each other about the five stages.

3. Put students into five groups.

4. Assign each group a stage of grief.

5. Using the Mask handout, markers, and any classroom materials available, have each group make a mask to represent the particular stage of grief they were assigned.

6. After each group has finished making their mask, place masks in the front of the room.

7. Ask one member from each group to come up in front of the room to share their mask. The student needs to include what stage the mask is representing.

8. Select another member from each group to come to the front of the room. The student will choose a mask other than the one he/she worked on making.

9. He/she will hold the mask up and discuss the thoughts and demonstrate the actions a person in this stage may display.

10. Give all students a chance to participate. Finish when all stages have been completed. If a student is unsure of the thoughts or actions that may be felt by someone in the stage of grief indicated by the mask, the student may get help from his/her group members.

Discussion Questions

1. How fast does it take an individual to pass through each stage?
2. What are some circumstances that complicate grieving?
3. What are the common threads of grief that students share when going through a loss?
4. How do you know when a person is through grieving?
5. How can you tell the stage of grief in which a person is currently functioning?
6. How comfortable were you when discussing the stages? Discuss your feelings.

Variations

- A maze may be used instead of a game to show there are many paths to acceptance of a loss.
- Allow students to entirely create their own masks, using whatever supplies are available in the classroom.
- Role plays may be used in place of the masks.
- Students may be given rehearsal time with their group members prior to showing the thoughts and actions of a person in the stage represented by the mask.

Take Five
Mask Handout

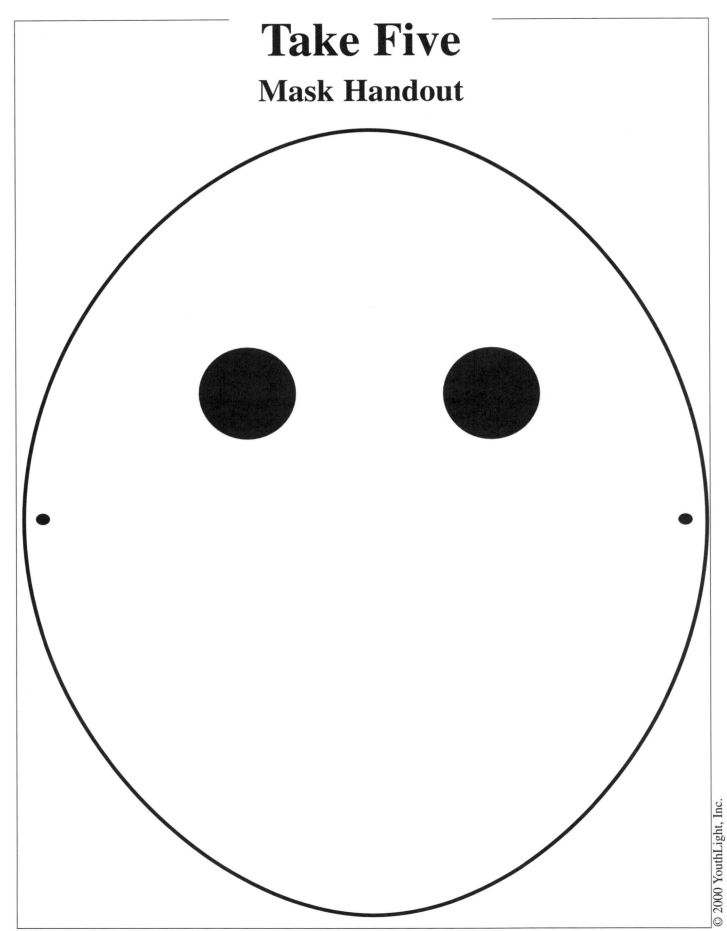

Take Five

Five Stages of Grief Handout

Denial   Failure to acknowledge the loss. Individuals appear in their normal state. No obvious changes in body language.

Anger   Get mad that the loss happened. Irritated facial expression, clenched fists, may kick things or show other signs of aggression.

Bargaining   Make a "deal" to bring person back. Pleading, question why person left instead of themselves or someone else.

Depression   Sadness. Mourn the loss of the way things were. Crying, sleeping all the time, change in eating habits, loss of interest in hobbies.

Acceptance   Realize that you can't change the situation…nothing will bring back that which was lost. Resuming normal activities. Normal moods of a person.

Date_____

Dear Parent/Guardian:

Today the students learned in "Take Five" the five stages of grief, the process the individual goes through while they are grieving, and the facial expressions, thoughts, and behaviors a person may display while in each stage of grieving.

It's important to become familiar with the stages of grief. Children will see loved ones experience loss(es) and will experience it for themselves as well. Understanding the stages and the way in which we move through the stages will help children understand themselves and where they or a loved one is in the process.

Listening is a giant role you've played throughout your child's life. It will be needed even more as loss is experienced. At home, you may wish to ask your child to explain the different stages to you. Ask your child to discuss how each stage is expressed. If your child has been through a loss or knows someone who has, you may want to personalize the discussion by telling how he/she or the other grieving person felt or behaved during the grieving process.

Sincerely,

_____

Life Plan

You may wish to send home permission notes for students to participate in this activity. You may also want to get permission from your supervisor concerning the religious element.

Objectives

Students will:

✔ identify ways people from different religious backgrounds grieve

✔ look for similarities in the ways people grieve

Materials Needed

"Life Plan for Grief" handout
"Ritualistic Steps of Grief" handout
Religious leaders and individuals who have lost a loved one who are willing to be interviewed by students (make sure interviewee understands role)
Pen or pencil

Procedures

Set up: Contact leaders of local religious sects to be interviewed regarding grief. Explain to leaders that they are to discuss ritualistic behaviors and emotions.

1. Give students the "Ritualistic Steps of Grief" handout.
2. Review the handout and explain that students are to take notes while religious leaders share information.
3. Put students into small groups. Have the students rotate from one religious leader to another until all students have seen each religious leader.
4. Have the students share the information they collected. Other students who are listening will add new information to their list. In addition, have the students place a check mark beside ritualistic steps that occur in all religions presented.
5. Pass out "Life Plan for Grief" handout. Explain the procedure. Do an example of cognitive, behavioral, and physical reactions as a class. (Behavioral - hitting, cognitive - this is awful, and emotional - sadness.)
6. The students will listen to individuals who have lost a loved one discuss their behavior, thoughts, and emotions concerning the loss. While listening, students will take notes.

Discussion Questions

1. What were the similarities between the ways the different religions grieved?
2. What thoughts and feeling came to mind as you were interviewing the individuals who had lost a loved one?
3. Which thoughts or feelings expressed by the survivors, have you experienced before?
4. How did you relate to some of the rituals as the religious leaders discussed grieving?
5. How is information on grieving passed on to the members of the religions?

Variations

- Allow students to go out in to the community and interview people from various cultures.
- Allow students to use the computer to research loss or death rituals of various cultures and share with their peers.
- Use sand, drama, or puppets to express the rituals or emotions involved in grieving.
- Have students discuss with their families the rituals they observe during a loss and share with each other.
- Play tic -tac- toe or another familiar game, when students lose, discuss how they would express the loss.

Life Plan
"Ritualistic Steps of Grief" Handout

Religion: _____

Ritualistic Steps: _____

_____

_____

_____

Religion: _____

Ritualistic Steps: _____

_____

_____

_____

Religion: _____

Ritualistic Steps: _____

_____

_____

_____

Religion: _____

Ritualistic Steps: _____

_____

_____

_____

Life Plan

"Life Plan for Grief" Handout

Emotional Reactions	Behaviors	Thoughts

Date_____

Dear Parent/Guardian:

In the "Life Plan for Grief" the students had an opportunity to hear the religious, behavioral steps associated with death. Students also interviewed individuals that have lost a loved one to find out possible behaviors, thoughts, and emotions associated with grief.

Death is an unfortunate part of all of our lives. By examining different religious groups students will better understand how society deals with death. The individuals interviewed helped the students develop an understanding for individual variations of grief.

Families are all unique and special. Each family has it's own way of dealing with grief and death. This may be an appropriate opportunity to discuss your family's ritualistic practices regarding death and grieving and to express the emotions which may be associated with loss. Discuss how through the generations, rituals have been passed down or have changed.

Sincerely,

_____

Coping to Survive

Objectives

Students will:

✔ generate a list of ways to cope with grief

✔ learn to meet the needs of a grieving person

Materials Needed

"Grief & Transition Scenarios" handout
Paper
Pencil

Procedures

1. Pass out the "Grief & Transition Scenarios" handout.

2. Have the students list what they would say to themselves or a friend who is experiencing the given scenario with the goal of allowing emotions to be expressed. Have them share their thoughts.

3. Have the students generate a list of activities that they enjoy and that help them to feel positive about themselves.

4. Next have the students state what they believe to be the needs of people who are going through grief or transition. This would be based on the interview with the individuals that had lost loved ones in the "Life Plan" activity and their own personal experiences.

5. The students should then match the activities they previously listed with the needs of a grieving person.

6. If all the needs are not met have them brainstorm with a partner on how they would fulfill those needs.

7. Have the class as a whole share their thoughts and additional activities.

Discussion Questions

1. Did you notice a strong tendency to react in one manner?
2. Why do some people react one way and some react differently?
3. Do certain scenarios affect your reactions? If so, which ones and how?
4. Did you use certain activities more than others to fulfill the needs of individuals going through grief or transition?
5. Do you perceive your needs when grieving or going through transitions to be different from other people?

Variations

• Take students to various types of environments where they are able to express appropriate and inappropriate behaviors. Have them role play these behaviors.
• Give a homework assignment using a diary at home to record coping activities.
• Have the students write a report on a grief experience that shows the activities they used to express and cope with grief.

Coping to Survive
"Grief & Transition Scenarios" Handout

Monday   I felt depressed and cried during social studies class.

Tuesday   I was sad. I went to my room because I wanted to be alone. I screamed into a pillow.

Wednesday   I kicked the wall in the ladies' restroom at a restaurant. I couldn't believe this was happening to me.

Thursday   "I'll do anything, " I said pleading. "Just bring my friend back," I sobbed.

Friday   Today I was quiet and hollow. I jogged by myself for hours. I just wanted to run until I couldn't feel anything anymore.

Date_____

Dear Parent/Guardian:

In the activity "Coping to Survive" the students were given "Grief & Transition Scenarios." From these scenarios they generated a list of ways to cope with transition or grief and how to meet the needs of the grieving person. The goal of this activity was to allow the grieving person to express their emotion. The students were also asked to make a list of activities they enjoy that help them feel positive about themselves. This list was then used to meet the needs of the grieving individual.

It is important for children to understand that it is necessary to express emotions during times of transition or grief. Through understanding they will allow themselves permission to grieve in the way they choose and to be more accepting of others' ways of coping. By learning to meet the needs of a grieving individual or one who is in transition, children find healthy ways to move on during a time of loss.

As a person who accepts your child, you are a natural to help your child accept his/her way of coping with a loss or transition. Help your child see his/her strengths and help him/her apply them in times of need.

Sincerely,

_____

Farewell

Objective

Students will:

✔ remember the positives they gained from having that which was lost

Materials Needed

Paper
Pen
Boxes
Gift wrap

Procedures

1. Talk to the students about the need to say goodbye and explain that this is a stage in grieving. Relay to them that saying goodbye often involves remembering the special events or times spent and expressing the joy that was given from that which was lost and the sadness at the loss.

2. Have the students write a letter addressed to that which was lost.

3. The students will place the letter in a box and gift wrap it.

4. Allow the students to decide if they wish to release the gift, and if so, how they will do that. (The students may decide to release the gift by taking the gift and giving it to family members of the person who has passed, they may put it on the grave, take it to a place they frequently shared with that which is lost, etc.) Students may also decide to hang on to the gift for a while. These students may keep the gift in their locker, book bag, bedroom, etc.

Discussion Questions

1. What do the box and the gift wrap symbolize?
2. Is saying goodbye necessary and why?
3. What effect does not releasing the box have?
4. How do you decide when to release the gift?
5. What happens after you release the box?

Variations

- Saying goodbye can be done in various ways. Poetry, role plays, music, writing stories, gift (or object) and drawing may be used in place of writing a letter.
- When working with individuals, stuffed animals may be used to tell someone goodbye.
- Students may keep a journal of their thoughts until they are ready to give the gift.
- The letter would not have to be placed in a box. It could be placed in any object that more closely symbolizes the relationship. (Examples: bury in the bottom of a plant, put in a shell, etc).

Date_____

Dear Parent/Guardian:

In the activity "Farewell" your child discussed the process of saying goodbye, which includes remembering the special qualities and times shared with that which was lost. Your child then formed these ideas into a letter, gift wrapped it, and chose whether to release the gift or hold on to it a while longer.

When your child is ready to say goodbye he/she is then moving towards acceptance. Everyone has their own special way of saying goodbye. It's important to allow your child to say goodbye in a way that is comfortable to him/her. I'm sure your warmth and support will continue as he/she expresses his/her feelings toward saying goodbye. It may be appropriate and comforting to share similar experiences you have had.

Sincerely,

_____

A Lofty Release

Objective

Students will:

✔ learn how to make the positives of their loss part of their current life.

Materials Needed

Balloons (one per child)
Helium tank
Index cards
Pens

Procedures

1. Give the students an index card. On one side of the card allow them to write down the positives about their losses.

3. On the other side of the card have them write their school address, so the card can be returned to them.

4. Allow the students an opportunity to share what they've written.

5. Give the students a balloon. Have them fold the index card up and place it inside the balloon. Next fill the balloon with helium and tie it.

6. As a group, have the students go outside and release their balloons.

Discussion Questions

1. How have you decided to make this loss a part of your life permanently?
2. Is it important to make the loss a part of your life? If so, why?
3. Would there be any instances where you would not want the loss to be part of your life?
4. What are some others ways you could incorporate this into your life?
5. How would you like to be remembered or incorporated into someone's life?

Variations

- Instead of using balloons, the students could put the message in bottles and release them.
- Have the students plant trees in memory of the loss and bury the letter in with the plant seeds.
- Suggest that the students find a new friend to share the same activities that they shared with the loss.

Date_____

Dear Parent/Guardian:

Today the students learned how to incorporate loss into their current lives through the "Lofty Release" activity. They wrote positive qualities about the thing or person that was lost and put those qualities in balloons to release them. If the message is found, the students school address is on the note. This allows the students an opportunity to connect with the person who finds the message and make a new friend.

Loss is a sad part of all life. With loss comes hope and renewal for new relationships. As your child works through the loss, he/she can start the process of initiating the new.

During times of loss your child will depend on you more than ever. You may discuss with your child how your family has incorporated loss into your life. Allow your child to share this new part of them.

Sincerely,

_____

Lifebowl

Objective

Students will:

✔ apply knowledge learned in Grief, Loss and Transition chapter

Materials Needed

10 empty one liter bottles with lids
1ball
"Lifebowl Questions"
Masking tape
Tape measure

Procedures

Set up: a. Using empty plastic bottles as pins, have the students stand at one end of the room with the pins at the other.

b. Mark with a piece of tape, the place where each pin will set. Pins should be in a triangular shape with a single pin at point nearest where the students will stand.

1. Divide class into two teams.

2. Choose a team to go first and a student from that team to go first.

3. The first team member takes the ball and rolls it toward the pins. The player tries to roll over as many pins as possible. If the student knocks over one pin, he/she must answer the first question in Lesson I, which has not been answered before during this game. If the student answers correctly, his/her team receives a point. If a student knocks over two pins, he/she must answer the first questions from Lesson 2, which has not been answered before in this game. Follow this pattern unless eight or more pins are knocked over with one roll. A student who knocks over eight pins with one roll, may choose from which lesson his/her question will be taken (lesson one through seven). A correct answer would still be worth one point. A student who knocks over nine pins, gets to choose from which lesson his/her question will be taken (lesson one through seven). A correctly answered question will be worth two points instead of one. If a student knocks over all ten pins he/she automatically gets two points and does not have to answer a question.

4. Teams take turns with rolling the ball and answering questions until all the questions have been examined.

5. The winning team is the one who scores the most points.

Discussion Questions

1. Do you have any questions about death, loss, grief, or grieving?
2. What have you learned from this chapter on Grief, Loss and Transitions?
3. How will you use what you have learned about grief and grieving?
4. Who experiences grief, loss and transitions?
5. Why do people experience grief differently?

Variations

• The number of points a student receives for answering a question correctly could be based on the number of pins he/she knocks over with one roll. Questions could then be asked progressively down the sheet of questions, with no regard given concerning from which lesson the questions were derived.

• Instead of bowling, baseball could be played, with a set number of points given for getting on each different base. Questions could then be asked progressively down the sheet of questions, with no regard given concerning from which lesson the questions were derived.

• Students could write their own questions and answers to each lesson. These questions could then be used to play a game or as a quiz or review.

• Several field day events such as the egg toss, water balloon toss, and the three-legged race could be used in place of bowling. A set of questions from one lesson will be matched to each event. The winner if the event will be given an opportunity to correctly answer the question and score a point for his/her team.

• Bowling, or any of the above mentioned events, could be made into individual rather than team events by keeping track of individual points.

Lifebowl
Questions

The correct answers to the questions listed below are located at the end of the question in parentheses.

Sticky Situation

1. Something you once experienced that is now no longer present is called a _____. (loss)
2. The emotions and process of adjustment after a loss has occurred is called_____. (grief)
3. Of the following which is not a loss: death, moving, growth, choosing to change jobs. (growth)
4. Everyone experiences a loss____. (T) or F
5. Give an example of a loss you've had in your life_____.

Life Raft

1. The way your body shows a loss is called a _____reaction. (physical)
2. What you do in response to a loss is called_____reaction. (behavioral)
3. Everyone cries when they experience a loss. T or (F)
4. Anger may be experienced as a result to loss. (T) or F
5. What is one emotional reaction to loss_____. (depression, sadness, anger)

Take Five

1. How many stages of grief are there? (five)
2. Which of the following is not one of the stages of grief: denial, (repression), anger, bargaining, acceptance, depression.
3. Denial is when you make a deal to bring the person back. T or (F)
4. When you reach _____ stage, then you no longer have to go back through the stages of grief anymore. (acceptance)
5. You may need to go through the stages of grief more than once. (T) or F

Life Plan

1. What are the three different ways people react to loss? (emotional, physical, behavioral)
2. There are differences in the way different religions deal with grief. (T) or F
3. Everyone experiences behavioral, emotional, and physical reactions when they grieve. T or (F)
4. List two common behavioral reactions that people have to loss. (possible answers: hitting, crying, screaming)
5. Give one emotional reaction that was similar in various religions. (sadness, anger)

Lifebowl
Questions

The correct answers to the questions listed below are located at the end of the question in parentheses.

Coping to Survive

1. People react differently to grief when they are placed in various scenarios. (T) or F
2. Coping means learning to manage your emotions. (T) or F
3. In which environment would a student be able to freely and appropriately express their anger associated with grief: school classroom, (counselor's office), school hallway, school cafeteria.
4. There is only one environment where everyone feels safe to express sadness. T or (F)
5. You can always manage the emotional, behavioral, and cognitive reactions to grief. T or (F)

Farewell

1. Nothing positive ever results from experiencing a loss. T or (F)
2. Saying _____ to a loss is important in reaching acceptance of the loss. (goodbye)
3. The only way to say goodbye to a loss is to attend a funeral. T or (F)
4. When saying goodbye to a loss, one only remembers all the sad times they experienced with that loss. T or (F)
5. Loss is inevitable...almost everyone will experience one type of loss at some point. (T) or F

Reincarnation

1. Once loss occurs, a person can never experience happiness again in his/her life. T or (F)
2. Which one of the following is a healthy example of how to make a loss part of one's life permanently: staying inside your house, dwelling on the sad aspects of the loss. (making new friends)
3. Writing messages, placing them in balloons and sending them up into the air is an example of _____ loss. (releasing)
4. Once you have accepted loss, it is healthy to make it a part of your life. (T) or F
5. Your family incorporates loss into their life the same exact way your best friend's family incorporates loss. T or (F)

Date_____

Dear Parent/Guardian:

Today we concluded the chapter on grief, loss and transitions. The students reviewed the skills they learned in previous activities by playing the game "Lifebowl."

Your child has learned skills to help him/her to cope with life's transitions and losses. Ask your child to share with you what he/she learned.

In the future, remember to use these skills during times of grief, loss and transition. Your child can help you and other family members find a healthy way to deal with life's ups and downs.

Sincerely,

_____

Chapter 4

Anger Management

I was angry with my friend;
I told my wrath, my wrath did end.
I was angry with my foe;
I told it not, my wrath did grow.
                    - William Blake

The goal of this chapter is recognizing anger, gauging levels of anger and managing anger. The chapter discusses the physical characteristics of anger, identifying anger, measuring the degree and frequency of anger, identifying behaviors as passive, aggressive or assertive, learning relaxation techniques, and using "I" messages.

Body Imaging

Objectives

Students will:

✔ define anger

✔ learn the physical characteristics of anger

✔ identify the "target" spots in his/her own body where anger is first displayed

Materials Needed

Long pieces of white paper (art paper or freezer paper work well)

Markers

Procedures

1. In small groups, have the students define anger.

2. As a class, have the students agree on one definition. (Anger may be defined as the feeling of extreme hostility, rage)

3. Next have the students close their eyes and visualize the last time they became very angry. Have them focus on how they felt. Ask what their stomach felt like, their head, eyes, etc. Now have the students focus on themselves externally. Ask them to visualize their face, neck, shoulders, arms, hands, legs, feet, etc. Tell them to get a clear, picture of what it felt like inside and how they looked outside. Now ask them to "freeze" this picture or store it firmly in their mind.

4. Now give each student a piece of paper that is long enough and wide enough for him/her to lay on and have his/her entire body on the paper.

5. Taking turns laying on the paper, have the students allow their partners to trace around their body.

6. Now have the students draw on the outline of themselves, the external and internal characteristics of their anger. (i.e. knots in stomach, clenched fists, grimace, clenched jaw, raised eye brows, etc.)

7. Share the drawings with the class.

8. Ask which of the characteristics they drew is usually the first thing they notice when they become angry. This is a "warning" or "target" characteristic for them that he/she is getting angry.

Discussion Questions

1. How does anger affect the way you feel inside?
2. What characteristics could tip you off that you are becoming angry or that someone else is angry?
3. What is it like when your body is going through its angry transformation?
4. How can you use this information about becoming angry?
5. What colors did or could you use to depict anger?

Variations

- You could have students cut physical characteristics of anger out of magazines.
- Students could make masks to display characteristics of anger.
- Puppets which show angry characteristics could be made.
- Students could do a sculpture of anger.
- Students could find an object that represents anger and share.

Date_____

Dear Parent/Guardian:

In the activity, "Body Imaging", the students defined anger and examined the physical characteristics which represent anger as well as the internal "feelings" of anger. To explore the characteristics and feelings, the students recalled a time when they were angry and then sketched a life-size body outline of themselves, complete with detailed characteristics of the feelings expressed.

With this activity the students were able to focus on the "warning" or "target" characteristics which told them when they were becoming angry. Once the students have identified the "warning" signs of anger, they can begin to monitor their behavior as they choose. Furthermore, this activity identifies the non-verbal clues of anger so that they may better identify anger in others. With this information, their communication skills grow.

You know your child better than anyone else. By using the "warning" signals of anger which were identified in the "Body Imaging" activity, you can help your child manage his/her behaviors as he/she so desires or needs. Ask your child to explain to you the external characteristics he/she displays when angry and how it feels inside to him/her. You may ask your child which of these physical characteristics or internal feelings is one of the first to appear when he/she becomes angry. This "symptom" could be used as a warning signal to your child to stop and think before reacting. All of us become angry. With "Body Imaging" you can help your child decide what to do with his/her anger.

Sincerely,

_____

Seeing "Red"

<table>
<tr><td>

Objective

Students will:

✔ identify situations that make him/her angry

</td><td>

Materials Needed

Construction paper
Pen
Markers
Chalk

</td></tr>
</table>

Procedures

1. Hand out a piece of construction paper to each student.

2. Ask the students individually to draw a picture of an event or situation that makes them angry. The students may draw in black or white or may use markers, etc.

3. Give the students time to draw.

4. Once the drawings are completed have them pair off into groups of two.

5. Have the pairs decide who will be first.

6. Next ask this student to "guess" what is going on in the picture their partner drew. What is making them angry?

7. Have them switch roles, where the other person guesses what is occurring in their partner's picture.

8. Randomly select students to share their pictures and what makes them angry.

9. List the situations or events that make them angry on the chalkboard.

10. Have the group as a whole discuss which situations listed they can relate to, as well as any additional events or situations that make them angry.

11. Discuss how different people feel angry after various situations.

Discussion Questions

1. Did you notice any specific events that "universally" were recognized as those that produced anger?
2. Did any event listed on the board affect you?
3. What type of situations seem to make you the angriest?
4. What are the specific reasons why some things make you angry while others do not?
5. Is there always one event that makes you angry no matter when it occurs?

Variations

- Instead of placing events on the board you may choose to record them on large pieces of construction paper taped around the room. You may randomly call on students to come up to these "charts" and write down the events that make them angry.
- Students may first discuss in small groups (instead of pairs) what makes them angry before discussing as a class. Students may also brainstorm all together as a class on what makes them angry.
- Cut out pictures from magazines or books of possible "upsetting" situations. Hold up the pictures at the beginning of class and have the students draw what events are going on in the pictures that may make someone angry. Videos may be used as well as puppetry to demonstrate and generate discussion on situations that cause anger. Sand play may be implemented with younger students to create a situation to show what makes them angry.
- Students may be asked to create a skit that shows an event that makes them angry, or may develop their own list of events that have caused them to be angry in the past.

Date_____

Dear Parent/Guardian:

With today's activity, "Seeing Red", the students learned how to identify what events or situations make them angry. They also learned that different people become angry following different events.

Identifying the feelings and emotions that lead to anger can help students recognize themes, times or persons around them that stir their anger. This is one step in determining what or who leads to anger. By being more aware, the students can begin to manage their anger.

Ask your child what events frequently cause him/her to become angry. Help your child identify his/her physical characteristics of anger by asking him/her what he/she is feeling when you suspect he/she is angry. For example, you may say, "I noticed your face is red and you are stomping your foot, are you feeling angry?" Helping your child become aware of his/her anger and when it occurs, takes him/her one step closer to independence and responsibility, a goal for which you have long strived!

Sincerely,

_____

Anger Thermometer

Objective

Students will:

✔ Learn to monitor and manage their anger

Materials Needed

Anger questionnaire handout
"Situation" handout
Measuring guide

Procedures

Set up: Tape the measuring guide to the floor.

1. Hand out the Anger questionnaire and allow the students time to complete the "Before" portion independently. Be sure to remind them that there are no right or wrong answers. These will be reviewed independently after the activity.

2. Explain how the measuring guide works (1=Never Angry, 2=Somewhat Angry, 3=Moderately Angry, 4=Very Angry, 5=Extremely Angry.

3. Read each "Situation" handout to the students. Have the students stand on the measuring guide to indicate how they would feel in each the given situation.

4. Have students pick up a small piece of paper each time they stand on the numbers 4 & 5.

5. After the students have chosen their spots, ask them how they came to that conclusion.

6. Once all the situations on the "Situation" handout have been read, have the students count the pieces of paper they have collected. Explain that the paper they have indicates how often they are "very" or "extremely" angry.

7. Now have the students fill out the "After" portion of the Anger questionnaire.

8. Discuss with them the outcome of the activity and their feelings about it.

9. Have them keep a journal for one week tracking how often they were angry. In the journal students may write what occurred before they became angry and how angry they became. Also have them explain how they handled their anger. (Be certain to share this at a later time.)

Discussion Questions

1. How did the students vary at different points on the anger line?
2. What did you learn from this activity?
3. How did you feel about where you were on the line?
4. What do you think it meant to have many or few pieces of paper. How do you feel about that?
5. What will you do with the information you have gained from this activity?

Variations

• Students may try counting to themselves when they are angry. The longer they count before becoming calm, measures how angry they really were.

• Students may be given a chart or other tangible item to mark or hold each time they become angry throughout the course of a day. (Paper clips made into a chain may work well.)

• Let students create their own visuals to show how angry they are. Example: an angry face that reaches an exploding stage, a staircase of anger (each step could labeled with what made them angry.)

• Play Dough® may be used to measure frequency and level of anger. Have the students break off a piece each time a situation in which they would become angry is read. The more anger they think they would experience, the larger the piece of Play Dough®. Through this variation they will be able to see their ball of Play Dough® grow. The Play Dough® may then be squeezed or smashed as a way to release the anger.

Anger Thermometer
"Anger Questionnaire" Handout

Before

1. How often do you become angry? (circle one)

Never   Almost never   Sometimes   Almost always   Always

2. How intense is your anger usually? (circle one)

Very low   Minor   Medium   Much   Extreme

3. In what ways do you handle your anger? (circle all that apply)

Screaming   Punching   Blaming   Talking calmly   Taking Responsibility   Doing Nothing

4. Would you like to change any of the following? (circle yes or no)

Yes or No   How often you become angry

Yes or No   The level of anger you feel at times

Yes or No   What you do when you're angry

After

1. How often do you become angry? (circle one)

Never   Almost never   Sometimes   Almost always   Always

2. How intense is your anger usually? (circle one)

Almost none   Minor   Medium   Much   Almost Complete

3. In what ways do you handle your anger? (circle all that apply)

Screaming   Punching   Blaming   Talk calmly   Take Responsibility   Do Nothing

4. Would you like to change any of the following? (circle yes or no)

Yes or No   How often you become angry

Yes or No   The level of anger you feel at times

Yes or No   What you do when you're angry

Anger Thermometer
"Situation" Handout

1. Your brother forgets to set the alarm clock and you miss your favorite Saturday morning tv program.

2. It is your turn to select a cereal at the store, but they are out of your favorite kind.

3. Your baseball game gets canceled because of rain.

4. You get out of your seat to go get a tissue when you get back your pencil is gone.

5. Someone calls you a name.

6. Your teacher tells you your answer is not correct.

7. Your brother tells your Mom you did something, but you did not do it.

8. Your art partner spills paint on your shoe.

9. You're the last one finished with your math test.

10. Your sister wears your favorite sweater without asking you.

Date_____

Dear Parent/Guardian:

Today, by participating in the activity, "Anger Thermometer" the students became aware of how often and to what extent they become angry. Each time an event or situation was read the students were to evaluate how they would feel. They measured their anger by standing on a measuring guide (1=Never angry to 5=Extremely angry) located on the floor.

Anger is a normal part of all our lives. However, if anger is a large part of a student's life or affects the student's daily interactions or functions substantially, the student may choose to do something about his/her anger.

It is natural to delight in your child's happiness. However, anger is a part of life. To gauge the extent of anger in your child's life you may monitor how often he/she becomes angry at home. Put a mark on a piece of paper each time he/she becomes angry for one evening or for each evening for a week. This will allow you and your child to have some data to use when examining whether anger is an area on which you wish to work. This may become a family activity by having everyone monitor him/herself or by just marking times when a "family" anger situation occurs. As a family, discuss your feelings regarding the data recorded and determine if attention needs to be given to this area.

Sincerely,

_____

Knock It Off

Objective

Students will:

✔ define and identify passive, aggressive, and assertive ways of dealing with anger

Materials Needed

"Definition/Role Play" handout
"Interview Question" handout

Procedures

1. Pass out the "Interview Question" handout and review it with the students.

2. Put the students in groups and allow them to interview one another.

3. Share the results of the interviews.

4. Discuss whether the answers were identical or different.

5. Pass out the "Definition/Role Play" handout to the students.

6. Read definitions of passive, aggressive and assertive.

7. Put the students in groups and assign one role play situation to each group. Explain that they must show an aggressive, an assertive and a passive way of reacting with their role play.

8. Allow the students time to rehearse the role plays.

9. Have the group present the role plays, with each of its reactions.

10. The students who are the audience for the role play will identify which reaction was passive, assertive, and which was aggressive.

11. Discuss the consequences of each reaction. As a group, decide which reaction would be the wisest.

Discussion Questions

1. What is the difference between aggressive and assertive behavior?
2. Is there one style (passive, aggressive, or assertive) that you use more often than the others?
3. What is the effect of using each of the styles?
4. What have you learned and how will you use this knowledge?
5. Is it important to be aware of your method of reacting or others method of reacting? If so, why and when?

Variations

- Put on a puppet show with the younger children.
- Use this information during physical education class to analyze the students physical behavior during competition.
- Discuss how each of these styles are used in the media.
- Use sand play as a means of expressing anger during play.

Knock It Off
"Definition/Role Play" Handout

Definitions

Aggressive : expressing in a pushy, offensive manner

Assertive: to express in a positive manner

Passive: not expressing a verbal response

Example: A new student is being picked on by other students.
Ways of reacting:
Aggressive - growl in the students' faces
Assertive - tell them you do not like it and ask them to stop
Passive - say nothing and do nothing

Role Plays

Situation #1   A student's parents tell him/her that he/she can only invite one friend to go to the roller skating rink with him.

Situation #2   A friend has the keys to his/her parents' car and want to go joy riding.

Situation #3   You want to go to the movies and your friend wants to go hiking.

Situation #4   Two friends disagree about what to get a third friend for his/her birthday.

Situation #5   A committee is discussing options to a problem and you feel you have a perfect solution.

Situation #6   You and your brother both want a brownie and there is only one left.

Knock It Off
"Interview Questions" Handout

Situation: You have an arm load of books and are headed for a nearby table. Someone gets to the table before you and sits down at the seat you wanted.

Question 1   How would you feel in the above situation?

Interviewee A: _____

_____

_____

Interviewee B: _____

_____

_____

Interviewee C: _____

_____

_____

Question 2   How strong would you react emotionally to this situation?

Interviewee A: _____

_____

_____

Interviewee B: _____

_____

_____

Interviewee C: _____

_____

_____

Question 3   What would you do in this situation?

Interviewee A: _____

_____

_____

Interviewee B: _____

_____

_____

Interviewee C: _____

_____

_____

Date_____

Dear Parent/Guardian:

In the activity, "Knock It Off" students identified and defined assertive, aggressive and passive ways of reacting to certain situations. The students applied this information to develop role plays and to make wise choices about their behavior when they become angry.

Understanding that there is more than one way to respond to any situation, even one which may evoke anger, gives your child the power to solve problems rationally in a manner that best befits him/her.

To help your child be aware of how he/she is reacting to anger, discuss his/her goal and the effectiveness of his/her choice in obtaining that goal. As a means of further examining possible ways to react and realizing the consequences of our choices, you and your child may examine other peoples choices for behavior and the effect it is having. This could even be done with situations on television. Keeping the lines of communication open will help your child continue to develop strategies for dealing with feelings.

Sincerely,

_____

Bubbling Over

Note: It may be appropriate to try this activity outdoors in a quiet area.

Objective

Students will:

✔ learn a relaxation technique

Materials Needed

Bubble solution
(may mix dish detergent and water)
Bubble wands, etc. (to make bubbles)
Cups

Procedures

1. Pass out a bubble wand and bubble mixture to each student. Give them an opportunity to enjoy making and observing the bubbles.

2. As the students are blowing bubbles, ask them to note how it feels to blow the bubbles.

3. As the students start, they can blow bubbles slowly, then faster and faster, trying to blow their anger away.

4. Have the students find a comfortable spot on which to sit.

5. Instruct them to relax, breathing in and out slowly.

6. Tell the students to think of one thing that makes them angry and to visualize blowing a big bubble. As they are blowing, they are to pretend that that which made them angry is inside the bubble.

7. Ask the students to watch this bubble float away and as it goes, so does their anger. If it bursts, their anger bursts too, or disappears.

8. Give the students additional time to blow bubbles and watch their anger float away.

9. As they begin to calm, have them focus on their slow, deep, concentrated breathing.

10. Give the students an opportunity to describe their experience verbally, in writing, or in an art mode.

11. Discuss how this relates to anger.

Discussion Questions

1. What was this experience like for you?
2. How did this activity affected you; Physically, Mentally?
3. What did you learn and how will you use this information?
4. When and where could you use this activity?
5. How could you modify this activity if you wanted to use it during your regular daily activities, when you become angry?

Variations

- Use any object students find comforting (i.e. feather, beach ball, flowing water, etc.)
- Teach the students deep breathing as a separate relaxation step that can be used anywhere anytime.
- Let the students generate relaxation scenarios that they want to pursue in a visualization.
- Use auditory stimulation in conjunction with slow, deep, controlled breathing.
- Let students make "angry" faces in a mirror until they are calm.

Date_____

Dear Parent/Guardian:

In "Bubbling Over", students participated in a relaxation activity. The students visualized their anger and then placed that anger in a bubble. The students breathed slowly as they let the anger in the bubble float away in their mind. Once the students were relaxed we discussed the anger and what they could do about it.

Learning to release anger so one can think calmly and rationally will set the stage for wise decision-making. Students need to learn that everyone becomes angry and that there are productive and acceptable ways to show that anger.

You may want to help your child practice relaxing on a regular basis and encourage its use when your son/daughter is becoming stressed or angry. Relaxation practice can be a healthy family activity.

Sincerely,

_____

I Spy

Objectives

Students will:

✔ identify messages that are "I" messages and those that are not "I" messages

✔ learn the importance of using "I" messages and how to communicate feelings with others

Materials Needed

"I Messages" handout
Construction paper
Pen
Pencils
Markers

Procedures

Set up: Before the students come into class, develop a skit with another teacher or counselor to act out in front of them. For example: A counselor enters the teacher's classroom to discuss the conflict mediation program. The counselor is upset because the teacher never allows his/her mediators to get out of class to mediate conflicts. A dialogue that may occur between the two may be as follows:

Counselor: "You never let my mediators out of your class to mediate conflicts. Our mediation program has not been that successful because you never work with us so the kids can mediate. Why are you not supporting us?"

Teacher: "Your mediators always have to miss my class or try to get out of it. They are missing class time and I am sick of you always thinking that they can make up their work whenever..."

1. When the students enter class begin a skit about a conflict such as the one suggested above.

2. Make sure the actors know to be accusatory and not to express their feelings behind their angry statements to each other.

3. After the skit, ask the class how the two actors expressed their anger in the conflict.

4. Ask the class if they know what an "I" message is.

5. Explain that an "I" message is a statement that conveys to the person thoughts and feelings behind the conflict. They are not merely just stating their anger, but are talking about the cause of the anger as well as the consequences and what they are feeling.

6. Randomly call on students to give examples of what would be an appropriate "I" message for the conflict that was demonstrated.

7. Pass out the "I" Message handout and have the students complete it.

8. End the lesson with the students handing each other the "I" messages written on the eyeball cutouts.

9. Generate a class discussion, if time permits, on the importance of using "I" messages.

Discussion Questions

1. Have you ever considered how you explain your feelings when in a conflict?
2. Do you notice that you already use "I" messages, and if so, are you able to develop them with ease?
3. How would you explain to a friend the value of using "I" messages?
4. Would there ever be a situation where "I" messages would not be appropriate or an effective means of conveying your thoughts and feelings?
5. Is there anyone you know in particular who is especially talented in developing or using "I" messages? If so, who, and what makes them so effective?
6. How do you spot when an eye message is being used clearly?

Variations

• Students can be given homework assignments the night before where they develop their own skits. In the skits, they have to show a conflict and show how they express their anger toward each other. The students may be placed in pairs or in small groups to accomplish this task.

• Divide the class into small groups and have students brainstorm the importance of using "I" messages by having them draw what would happen if "I" messages were not used. The students may use books or magazines to get ideas about how people express anger.

• Have students observe for a day or interview how other people convey their anger, thoughts and feelings toward others.

I Spy
"I Messages" Handout

Of the following ten statements, circle the sentences which contain "I" messages.

1. I feel hurt that you called me names because it makes me feel as though you do not want to be my friend anymore.

2. Why did you have to yell at me in front of all of my friends, anyway?

3. What made you decide to go to the movies with Sally instead of going with me?

4. I was really bothered today when you decided to sit with those other girls at lunch because I thought we had planned to sit together today and I was disappointed by the whole situation.

5. I can't believe you passed the test and I didn't after you helped me study for it.

6. I feel bad that I can't meet today to work on our school project because I made a committment to it and now I feel as though I have let you down.

7. I am really frustrated because I worked a long time on that project and now I feel as though you have taken all the credit for it.

8. I feel upset because I have been sick and have missed so much school and now I am really falling behind in my work. I hope I will be able to catch up in time before progress reports are ready to be sent to my parents.

9. You are always talking to my friends and now they don't want to even talk to me any more.

Date_____

Dear Parent/Guardian:

In today's activity, "I Spy" the students learned the elements of an "I" message and how to use it to share their feelings and thoughts with others. With this method of communication, students must take responsibility for their feelings and thoughts. Students beginning sentences with "I" and focus on how the situation makes them feel.

Listening to your child is a big part of parenting. "I" messages help make this easier by helping your child learn the process of talking about his/her feelings. Talk to your child about how he/she expresses his/her feelings when angry. Encourage your child to practice using "I" messages with family members.

Sincerely,

_____

Laughing at Anger

Objective

Students will:

✔ learn creative solutions to problems which could be stressful or lead to anger

Material Needed

"Situations" Handout

Procedures

1. Tell students to think of an old porcelain bathtub. If necessary, show them a picture of one.

2. In groups, have students create as many ideas for its use as possible. Be sure to tell them not to rule out any ideas, regardless of how silly or impossible an idea may sound.

3. Share the ideas as a whole class and have the students discuss. Which ideas were funniest and why.

4. Give students the hand out of situations and in a group have them generate as many ideas as possible for solving the situation. Be sure to tell them to be creative and not rule out what may seem silly. Also be sure to tell them that solutions where people or property are damaged will not be accepted.

5. Let students discuss ideas and vote on most humorous solution for each situation.

6. Define consequence as being that which could happen as a result of another action. Discuss the consequences of using the most humorous solutions, as well as other solutions.

7. Talk with students about humor and using it as a choice.

Discussion Questions

1. How did you feel about this activity?
2. Was this activity easy, somewhat difficult or hard for you? What made it this way for you?
3. Could you use this procedure when you are angry? Why or Why not?
4. For those solutions you found to be funny, what made them funny?
5. What did you learn from this activity and how will you use it?

Variations

- The students could dramatize or draw solutions.
- Invite the students to use this method the next time they are angry and write a journal entry or share with the class the results of their attempt. They should comment about what their thoughts were at the time and how these did or did not make it possible.
- Have the students practice deep breathing ideas from the previous lesson before attempting to be creative or humorous.
- Use the students' real life problems when brainstorming.

Laughing at Anger
"Situations" Handout

1. Your parents aren't home when you arrive after school and you forgot your key.

2. Someone at school says you were looking at his/her paper during a test. You were not.

3. Someone walks by your desk, hits it, and knocks everything off.

4. The principal asks to see you in the office.

5. You wanted the teacher to choose you to help hand out papers.

6. You asked your parents for a new bike for your birthday, but didn't get it.

7. You did poorly on a test.

8. Someone says you're stupid.

9. You're chosen last to be on a team for a softball game.

10. You left your completed homework at home.

Date_____

Dear Parent/Guardian:

Students were encouraged to see the humorous side of things in our activity, "Laughing at Anger." Students practiced creating solutions to problems that were potentially stressful and may lead to anger for some. In groups, students listed many options to a problem situation. Students thought of all possibilities including ideas that were unusual or creative.

We all have problems. How we view them is up to us.

Challenge your child to see problems in a less serious manner. Your goal can be to help your child realize there is more than one solution and more than one emotion related to problems. This could easily be done as a family activity. List some problems family members have experienced and begin generating possible solutions. Allow members to contribute ideas even if they may sound odd. Practice different strategies together. In any case, try to relax and have fun!

Sincerely,

_____

Anchoring Your Anger

Objective

Students will:

✔ apply the information gained from the Anger Management chapter

Material Needed

"Anger Management Questions"

Procedures

1. Put students into three teams. Explain that the objective of the game is to get the most points by answering questions correctly.

2. Choose a team and a player form that team to go first.

3. This player chooses a point value (5 points, 10 points, 15 points, or 25 points) for which he/she wishes to attempt. Be sure to tell the students that the higher the point value for which they are striving, the more difficult the question, and if they do not answer the question correctly, they get no points.

4. Read the first question with the chosen point value from the "Anger Management Question." The student then has one minute to answer. If the student answers correctly, he/she receives the number of points he/she chose. (If the student does not answer the question correctly, do not give the correct answer so the question may be used again later. If the student answers the question correctly, do not ask the same question again.

5. Alternate from team to team answering questions.

6. The game is over when all the questions are answered or after a predetermined amount of time is established.

7. The winner is the team with the highest number of points.

Discussion Questions

1. How do you identify thoughts that make you angry?
2. What is the difference between an aggressive, a passive, and an assertive way to deal with anger?
3. How would you describe "I" messages?
4. How do you talk with an angry person?
5. What are some of the ways your body responds to anger?
6. How does relaxation affect anger?

Variations

- Have the students spin a spinner to determine which category their question will be taken from instead of letting them choose their category. They may still choose the point value of their question from that category.
- Students may play a Bingo type game. Assign each question a number and letter, then make up cards with various numbers and letters on them. Pass the cards out and play the game.
- Make a dart game using darts with suctions on the end. Have each section of the dart board pertain to a lesson. Students will receive the point value from the space in which their dart landed if questions are answered correctly.

Anchoring Your Anger
"Anger Management Questions"

The correct answers to the questions listed below are located at the end of the question in parentheses.

Body Imaging

10 Points	Anger is	

 a. a feeling of great joy
 (b.) a feeling of extreme hostility or rage
 c. a feeling of being alone

5 Points   (T) or F   Clenched fist could be a characteristic of anger.

5 Points   (T) or F   People express anger in different ways.

5 Points   T or (F)   There are some people who never experience anger.

10 Points   What are the "warning signals" that you are becoming angry? (Accept all reasonable answers)

Seeing Red

5 Points   T or (F)   All people experience anger at the same time?

5 Points   (T) or F   Everyone experiences anger at some point in their lives.

10 Points   Learning how to control your anger is called _____. (anger management)

5 Points   (T) or F   People deal with anger differently.

5 Points   (T) or F   You choose how you will react to anger.

Anger Thermometer

5 Points   T or (F)   Everyone always becomes very angry when someone calls them a name.

5 Points   T or (F)   There are never any differences in how angry a person becomes.

5 Points   (T) or F   Some people become angry more often than others.

15 Points   Anger _____ means how angry a person is. (level)

15 Points   Anger _____ means how often a person becomes angry. (frequency)

Anchoring Your Anger
"Anger Management Questions"

The correct answers to the questions listed below are located at the end of the question in parentheses.

Knock It Off

25 Points   Expressing your anger in a positive way is called _____ .(assertive)

25 Points   Ignoring another student's negative comments is a _____ way of dealing with a situation. (passive)

25 Points   Expressing anger in a pushy, offensive manner is an _____ way of reacting. (aggressive)

5 Points   (T) or F   People often use one way of reacting more frequently than the others.

5 Points   T or (F)   Everyone placed in a given situation will react the same way.

Bubbling Over

15 Points   In the activity when we blew bubbles, what did we visualize was inside the bubbles? (That which had made us angry.)

15 Points   During the visualization exercise, when the bubble burst, what happened to the anger? (It was released.)

10 Points   _____ is when we are not stressed or strained. We are calm. (Relaxed)

5 Points   (T) or F   We can relieve ourselves of anger.

10 Points   Which of the following was not one relaxation method we discussed?
   a. blowing bubbles
(b.)hitting others
   c. slow, deep concentrated breathing

I Spy

15 Points   _____ are statements that convey both thoughts and feelings about a conflict to the listener. ("I" messages)

5 Points   T or (F)   We always use "I" messages every time we try to explain how we feel to someone else who is involved in the situation.

Anchoring Your Anger
"Anger Management Questions"

The correct answers to the questions listed below are located at the end of the question in parentheses.

5 Points   (T) or F   "I" messages are statements that usually begin with the pronoun I.

5 Points   T or (F)   It is always easy to use and develop "I" messages when trying to explain how you feel about a situation.

Laughing at Anger

5 Points   T or (F)   You should rule out silly or unusual ideas when creatively generating solutions.

15 Points   A _____ is that which could happen as a result of another action. (consequence)

5 Points   (T) or F   Getting put in time out could be a consequence.

10 Points   Give a solution to the following scenario. You are running late for school and you can not find your shoes. (Accept all reasonable answers)

5 Points   (T) or F   When choosing how to react to situations, one should consider the consequences of each reaction.

Date_____

Dear Parent/Guardian:

In "Anchoring Your Anger" the students were given the opportunity to "anchor" their anger or manage it, by applying the skills they learned throughout this chapter.

Although all of us get angry at times, we make different choices about what to do with our anger. Learning effective methods of managing anger can make one's life more relaxed and worry free.

You can continue to be there for your child through encouraging awareness and growth. Ask your child to apply the techniques he/she has learned when angry feelings arise.

Sincerely,

_____

Chapter 5

Conflict Resolution

All your strength is in your union.
All your danger is in discord;
Therefore be at peace henceforward,
And as brothers live together.
- Henry Wadsworth Longfellow

The goal of conflict resolution is to help students see disagreement as a part of life to be dealt with in a rational, logical manner. It is our goal that this process will become automatic and will supersede the flight or fight instinct. This unit incorporates interpreting body language, analyzing point of view and its effect, employing team work and depending on others to achieve a goal, using problem solving skills and listening skills into the process of conflict resolution and mediation.

Conflict Conclusions

Objective

Students will:

✔ learn that conflict is inevitable and part of life

Materials Needed

Pen
Pencil
Paper
Easel or blackboard
"Conflict Brainstorming" handout

Procedures

1. Have the students sit in a circle.

2. Write the word conflict on the board or easel.

3. Ask the students individually to draw a picture of a conflict. This can be a conflict in general, or one in which they have experienced.

4. Randomly select a student to call out the first word that comes to his/her mind when looking at the picture of their conflict.

5. Record the student's word on the board or easel near the word conflict.

6. Go around the room by continually calling on the next student to call out a word that represents the conflict. Be sure not to cue them in any positive or negative way as to the kinds of words they may say. Move quickly from student to student.

7. Record each student's response on the board or easel, placing the words around the word conflict.

8. Continue until all students have had a chance to respond with a word that represents conflict.

9. Pass out the "Conflict Brainstorming" handout and have the students individually complete it.

10. Generate a classroom discussion. Ask the class how conflict is viewed in general. Discuss the positive and negative words related to conflict. Explain to the class that conflict is an inevitable part of life. Conflict is a chance to learn about themselves.

Discussion Questions

1. What kinds of words came to mind immediately when they thought of the word conflict?
2. What feelings did these words generate when they were looking at their pictures?
3. Were some words positive or negative? Were they uncomfortable by nature?
4. Where did you learn the meaning of conflict?
5. Has your definition of conflict changed since doing this activity?
6. What words were most frequently stated when the word conflict was written on the board?
7. How can you learn to view conflict differently in your life?
8. Has anyone ever escaped conflict entirely?

Variations

- Students may write down words that represent conflict individually instead of going around the room in a group.
- Students may be placed in pairs, share what conflict means to them and what words come to their minds.
- Students may be divided into teams where one team is responsible for developing negative words that represent conflict, while the other team develops positive words that represent conflict.
- Ask the students to role play a conflict, generate words related to it. Write an essay on how conflict may be an opportunity to learn in their lives.
- Bring in songs, tapes, CDs and play tunes that may depict conflicts going on in the artists' lives. Ask students what the artist is trying to say about conflict.

Conflict Conclusions
"Conflict Brainstorming" Handout

Which words come to your mind first when you think of the word conflict? Circle those words. Put an N next to those words which appear negative, and a P next to those that appear positive.

_____ resolution		_____ urgency
_____ sadness		_____ problem
_____ agreement		_____ enemy
_____ depression		_____ accountability
_____ anger		_____ mediation
_____ change		_____ blame
_____ guilt		_____ dishonesty
_____ distress		_____ violated
_____ ending		_____ bitter
_____ resentment		_____ fairness
_____ mad		_____ equality
_____ fight		_____ difficult
_____ opportunity		_____ taxing
_____ growth		_____ draining
_____ beginning		_____ hope
_____ fear		_____ exhausting
_____ anxiety		_____ relentless
_____ envy		_____ forgiving
_____ jealousy		_____ negative
_____ renewal		_____ positive
_____ solutions		_____ sabotage
_____ argue		_____ peace
_____ yelling		_____ fluctuating
_____ misunderstanding		_____ emotional
_____ understanding		_____ inflexible

Date_____

Dear Parent/Guardian:

In the activity, "Conflict Conclusions" the students discovered through class discussion, how they viewed conflict. They were asked to write words on the board that represented their definition of conflict. We then discussed how conflict is perceived, while questions were answered concerning how conflict is viewed in general.

Your child learned that conflict is an inevitable and normal part of life. He/she learned that ultimately, conflict is a chance to learn and grow and make positive changes throughout life. Learning to cope with everyday, as well as situational conflict, your child continues to grow intellectually and emotionally.

Continue setting positive examples on how to handle conflict. Your child will appreciate your support, and may therefore reduce any possible stress or uncertainty which could accompany making decisions when dealing with conflicts. You may examine what conflict means to your child and as a family in general. Each family has their own unique perspective on how to cope with conflict. How do you view conflict? Ask your child how conflict can be used in a positive way in your family and in his/her individual development.

Sincerely,

_____

Getting the Big Picture

Objectives

Students will:

✔ learn, use and interpret body language to communicate

✔ define and experience the affects of different points of view

Materials Needed

Pictures of people selected from *Life* or a comparable magazine

Procedures

1. Define the phrase "point of view" (what one sees from a given perspective).
2. Show the students one eighth of the picture you have selected. Have them discuss what they notice, what emotions, if any are shown and what they think that part of the picture is showing.
3. Gradually show the students more of the picture. Allow the students time to discuss and predict what the picture is.
4. As you reveal the picture, ask the students what causes their answers to change.

Discussion Questions

1. What did you learn and how will you use it?
2. How did your point of view change as more of the picture was revealed?
3. How will you use point of view in conflict resolution?
4. Which emotions were the easiest to guess from body language?
5. Do we need to be aware of body language and if so, why?

Variations

- Write the following emotions on separate pieces of paper(sad, happy, angry, surprised, frustrated, excited, afraid, lonely). Place the pieces of paper in a container. Allow students to draw out an emotion. Whatever emotion students draw out they will act out while others try to guess the emotion. As students guess the emotions, discuss the clues given by the actor and the accuracy of the clues.

- Use several copies of the same picture which have varying degrees of clearness. Instead of revealing only a portion of the picture, show the least clear portion of the picture to the most clear picture.

- Students may do drawings of each of the emotions, instead of charades.

- Put an object which has very different characteristics on each of its sides on a raised piece of glass. Have students observe the object from different positions in the room (under the object, above the object, from the right, from the left, etc.). As they observe the object from each position, have them stop and describe only what they have seen so far. (A die could be used here. Depending on one's perspective a different number will have been rolled.)

Date_____

Dear Parent/Guardian:

Today in class the students participated in an activity called "Getting the Big Picture." Through this activity they were asked to define, examine and discuss the affects of different perspectives.

As a parent you may constantly see how your child's perspective on a situation may differ from yours. Continue keeping an open mind when listening to his/her views, while realizing that there are not necessarily any right or wrong views, but merely different points of view. While listening to your child's view, acknowledge that although you may disagree sometimes, it's OK to have a different perspective. Having different perspectives will allow your child to expand his/her knowledge and awareness of people's thoughts and feelings. In turn, compassion and tolerance for others may be developed.

Encourage your child to pay attention and be open when listening to other's perspectives. Keep in mind how body language plays a large part in conveying and truly hearing what the speaker is trying to say. Practice discussing with your child different perspectives by developing scenarios such as filling a glass halfway and seeing how he/she perceives its meaning. Another suggestion is to watch a movie with your child, stop the movie right before the ending and discuss what you both think the ending will be to see how your perspectives match or differ.

Sincerely,

_____

Team Building

Objectives

Students will:

✔ learn to work as a team

✔ learn to depend on others in order to achieve a goal

Materials Needed

Several sheets of paper
Scissors
Tape
Watch or timer

Procedures

1. Put students into groups of three.

2. Explain to the students that they will be making paper chains. The three steps to making a chain is: 1) cut the strips, 2) wrap the paper into a link, 3) tape the link. For a chain to be considered complete, it must have at least three links.

3. Allow the students three minutes to plan their work.

4. Give them their supplies.

5. Allow five minutes to work.

6. Count the number of chains each team completed in the five minutes.

7. The team who made the most chains is the winner.

Discussion Questions

1. What role does team work play on conflict resolution?
2. What was easy or difficult about this activity?
3. If you were to participate in this activity what would you do differently next time?
4. What do you think of how your team used their planning time?
5. What have you learned and how will you use it?

Variations

- Give the students a timed task that encourages them to work as a team to conquer the situation. An example could be using a trust fall exercise. Students must form a line and have one person stand at the head of the line and have other team members catch him/her while they fall into the line. Students must work together to make sure the falling student does not actually fall onto the ground.

- The students may also be taken outdoors to a park and be given directions on how to build a campfire, and how to set up a tent. This will encourage team work while the students themselves figure ut how to accomplish the procedure while the facilitator is watching.

- Instead of using chains of paper use popcorn to make the strands.

Date_____

Dear Parent/Guardian:

In the "Team Building" lesson today, the students focused on working together as a team, in order to learn to depend on others. Students were given the task of making a paper chain link. They were given three minutes in which to plan how to develop the link, and then were given five minutes to complete the task.

Team building and working together are important, vital elements your child will need to develop to succeed and enhance their lives. Your child may encounter situations where he/she must work together with others in a school or work setting, as well as in a social situation. Learning to be an effective and energetic team player will help your child develop confidence and positive work morale.

Your support in demonstrating to your child at home how working together in your family may help develop skills he/she may use outside the home and in other situations in life. Ask your child to give examples of how the family works together to help each other during times of stress. How can he/she change or improve skills to be more effective team participants in the family? Give specific examples to your child of opportunities he/she can take that would develop team building skills for the family and outside the home. Working together as a family promotes tolerance and compassion. These qualities will enhance his/her social skills throughout life.

Sincerely,

_____

Party Time

Objectives

Students will:

✔ learn the similarities between themselves and others

✔ use problem solving skills to make decisions as a group.

Materials Needed

Pen or pencil
"Party Planner" handout

Procedures

1. Pass out the "Party Planner" handout.

2. Allow the students time to see what choices they would make and list them on the handout for planning the party.

3. Give them time to mingle together, searching for others in the class who have similar party items listed. Students will use their handout and put the classmates name beside the category that they answered in a similar manner.

4. Ask the students to raise their hands to determine how many people fit into each category on the handout.

5. Discuss the steps to problem solving. (List the choices, consider needed consequences, choose an option, reflect)

6. List the ways that a decision can be made when there is a disagreement. Examples may include flipping a coin, picking a number, voting, etc.

7. Put the students in groups. Have the students come to a consensus for each area of the handout.

8. Allow the students to share their plans for their party.

Discussion Questions

1. What was it like to find classmates who answered the questionnaire in a similar manner to how you answered it?
2. What was the most difficult thing about planning the party?
3. How did you feel about planning the party with a group?
4. What have you learned and how will you use it?
5. Which problem solving step is the most helpful and why?
6. If you were planning the party with a group again, would you do anything differently? If so, what?
7. Do you think working with another group would be easier or harder? Why?

Variations

- Allow the students to generate a real life problem that is common to all of them and solve it as a group.
- Allow the students an opportunity to work with other groups and discuss their experiences?
- Have the students plan a time and group with which they will use these skills, then share their experiences with the class.
- This activity can be used to set up classroom rules, consequences, and rewards, instead of planning a party.
- This activity may also be tied to social studies and a mock legislative session could be conducted where problem solving and decision making skills are used.

Party Time
"Party Planner" Handout

Food

_____

_____

_____

_____

_____

Music

_____

_____

_____

_____

_____

Location

_____

_____

_____

_____

_____

Guests

_____

_____

_____

_____

_____

Decorations

_____

_____

_____

_____

_____

Games/Activities

_____

_____

_____

_____

_____

Time

_____

_____

Time

_____

_____

Time

_____

_____

Date_____

Dear Parent/Guardian:

Today we learned to make decision making skills in the activity "Party Planner." The students were asked to design a party with all the elements that go in throwing a party. The students had to make decisions on where to hold the party, what decorations to bring, who to invite, what food to have, what time to have the party, etc. They had to make decisions about the party as a group.

Your child at some point will have to work with others when making decisions in planning for events. This may occur during school events, future work events, projects, or social parties. Through much planning and decision making, your child will realize the he/she may agree and disagree with others. Similarities and differences between self and others is part of learning to make decisions together.

Your positive attitude toward accepting similarities and differences between your child and others may promote a pleasant work ethic and demeanor when planning events. Allow your child the opportunity to have a part in planning events at home. When obstacles occur, ask him/her how the differences can be dealt with effectively. What improvements can be made? Please stress to your child that planning activities can be a rewarding experience despite obstacles that come along with the process.

Sincerely,

_____

Work It Out

Objectives

Students will:

✔ learn to solve a problem by themselves

✔ learn to solve the same problem with a partner

Materials Needed

Pen or pencil
Paper
Chalk
Chalkboard

Procedures

1. Have the students write about a problem they have experienced within the last five years. They should also include their explanation of the problem.

2. List and explain the following steps to problem-solving.
   State the problem
   List choices
   Generate possible consequences of each choice
   Choose an option
   Reflect on choice

3. Have them write a solution to the following problem.
   Problem: You're at a party and one of the guests passes out.

4. Pair the students.

5. Have the students discuss their solutions to the problem.

6. If their solutions differ, they should come up with a joint solution.

7. Allow the pairs time to share their solutions with the class, stating their response to each problem-solving step.

8. As a class, solve the following problem using the problem-solving steps.
   Problem: Several students have been told by a classmate, that he plans to cheat on a final examination. The student needs to pass the test to be promoted to the next grade level.

Discussion Questions

1. What is the value in using the steps to problem solving?
2. Which took longer and why - solving a problem independently or with a partner?
3. What is the value of solving a problem with others?
4. How can you incorporate the problem-solving method into your life?
5. Does a solution become obvious when using the problem-solving method?
6. What is the importance of generating more than one solution to a problem?
7. What is the importance of reflecting on one's choice to a problem.

Variations

- Show a film or news clip and stop it to problem-solve about what has occurred.
- Tie problem-solving to current events, and role play being the persons involved in disputes.
- Use mystery books, and problem-solve "who done it."
- Have students list problems that are occurring in their school and use the problem-solving method to generate solutions.
- Have students lead a problem-solving session where participants are inexperienced in the problem-solving method.
- Have the students watch TV sitcoms. In the first 15 minutes have the watch the decision/problem, that needs to be addressed. Then ask them what the characters on the TV show did to solve the problem.

Date_____

Dear Parent/Guardian:

Your child learned problem-solving steps in "Work It Out", an activity we did today in class. He/she experienced solving problems independently, with a partner, and as part of a large group. We discussed the value of using the problem-solving process.

While your child is learning the steps to the problem solving process, he/she is developing skills that will be useful throughout life. Your child will encounter problems along life's path, both large and small. Effectively learning how to resolve them, methodically, will promote greater self-confidence in your child.

As a parent it's difficult to watch your child struggling to resolve problems. With your continual positive support, you may watch your child flourish as he/she becomes more confident when rectifying problems. Ask your child to explain to you the steps to problem-solving. You may use these steps with your child when you and he/she disagree. The steps may also be used when you child is disagreeing with another family member such as a sibling.

Sincerely,

_____

Wheel of Conflict

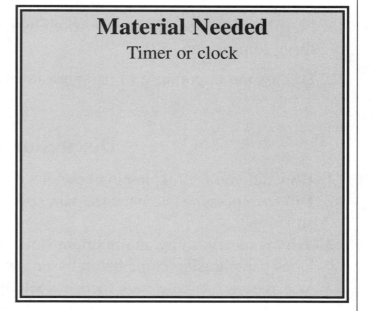

Objectives

Students will:

✔ learn to hear thoughts and feelings implied in a message

✔ learn the importance of paraphrasing

Material Needed

Timer or clock

Procedures

1. Ask the students the definition of paraphrasing. Discuss what it means.

2. Explain you will be developing a paraphrase wheel.

3. Ask the students to count off by ones and twos (1,2,1,2…). Continue until everyone has been counted.

4. Ask all the students with the number one to stand and form a circle in the middle of the room. They should be facing out.

5. Ask all the members of team two to stand and form a circle around the number ones in the center of the room. Make sure they are facing in toward the number ones so that the students are now looking at each other.

6. Explain that everyone is to think of a continuing conflict going on in their lives. Give them two minutes to brainstorm individually.

7. Tell the members of team two that they will be discussing their conflicts first by telling their stories to the number ones they are facing in the circle.

8. Allow 3 minutes for them to tell their story.

9. After the number twos have told their stories, have the number ones take 3 minutes (timed) to paraphrase back what they just heard.

10. Now have each member of team two move one person to their right. Continue the process again. Do this until all the number twos have moved and explained their story 3 times to 3 different people to their right.

11. Now have the ones and twos switch by making the inner circle the outer circle and so forth. Repeat steps 7-9.

12. Discuss the importance of paraphrasing as a class.

Discussion Questions

1. How did you feel explaining your story three times to three different people?
2. Did each person state back the same perspective or thoughts and feelings about your situation?
3. Why is paraphrasing an important skill to learn?
4. Does paraphrasing come naturally or is it an acquired skill?
5. Was it easier to state back facts or feelings regarding the conflict?
6. Did each person's perspective on your conflict bring forth new ideas concerning what your conflict really is?
7. What is your definition of paraphrasing?

Variations

- Have the students individually and then as a class come up with conflicts where they can then paraphrase each others messages.
- Develop a simple handout with conflicts leaving them ample room to write out a paraphrase to that conflict. The students may be placed in groups for this variation.
- The students may develop their own conflicts and paraphrases and then present them to the class by developing skits.
- Have one group of students state facts about a conflict, while another group states feelings concerning the conflict. Have a third team develop paraphrases to the conflict including both fact and feelings.
- Divide the class into teams. Make up conflicts and have the students pick one from a hat. Have "mini" paraphrase wheels going around the room, but having only one person stating that conflict three times. At the end each team has one person share their paraphrase with the class. As a class hold a contest to see which wheel most accurately gives an effective paraphrase.

Date_____

Dear Parent/Guardian:

In the activity, "Wheel of Conflict" the students learned how to paraphrase thoughts, feelings, and facts when listening to peer's conflicts. They also learned the importance of paraphrasing and that it requires practice to become proficient.

Your open and supportive manner in communicating with your child will help him/her become more confident in speaking with others. Paraphrasing is not a skill that comes naturally, rather, it's one that needs continual practice and development. By learning to paraphrase the thoughts and feelings behind the words given in a story, your child will have a better understanding of what the other person is trying to communicate. Paraphrasing is a skill needed throughout your child's life.

You may wish to discuss how your child and family communicate messages and conflicts to one another. A discussion on how each family member understands each other's conflicts may occur. Practice sending back messages to your child by describing his/her thoughts, feelings and facts. Work hard to focus in on what message your child is trying to convey.

Sincerely,

_____

Negate the Issue

Objective

Students will:

✔ learn the steps for mediation

Materials Needed

"Rules for Mediation" handout
"Styles of Conflict Resolution handout
"Conflict Mediation Process" handout
Pen
Paper

Procedures

1. Ask the class to define conflict resolution.

2. Discuss what mediation is in relation to conflict resolution.

3. Pass out the "Rules for Mediation" handout. Go over each ground rule for participation, respect, support, and confidentiality until *all* students understand them.

4. Pass out the "Style of Conflict Resolution" handout. Discuss how people handle conflict in different ways by giving examples of these styles as a class. Write them on the board.

5. Divide the class into teams containing 4 students per team. Explain that they will be learning the basic steps to mediating a conflict. Pass out the "Conflict Mediation Process" handout to each team member. Review by writing the steps on the board.

6. Have the teams develop a conflict and then go through the steps. Two students begin as mediators while the other two are in a conflict. Have them switch roles.

7. Call upon a group to come in front of the class to role play their conflict and to show the mediation steps to the class.

8. Have each group develop their own method for teaching the mediation steps. They may make up songs, use acronyms, rhymes, pneumonic devices, etc. to teach each other the steps to mediation.

9. Have each team come to the front of the class to demonstrate and teach their method and share their steps to mediation.

10. Ask a group to volunteer at another time, to teach a different class the steps of mediation.

11. As a class discuss the importance of using the mediation steps toward working through a conflict.

Discussion Questions

1. Are mediation and conflict resolution the same thing?
2. Which steps are the most difficult to master when using mediation?
3. Is mediation a comfortable means for resolving conflicts for yourself? If not, explain why.
4. Would you recommend other students to use a mediation program in a school if one is developed?
5. Do you feel comfortable discussing your conflicts with your peers?
6. Do you feel mediation promotes positive outcomes and solutions to conflicts?

Variations

- Mediation skills may be taught to students individually or in groups. Basic attending skills may also be taught as an introduction to the mediation process.
- Certified mediators may be brought into the class to present and demonstrate the mediation process. They may also discuss the difficulties and and answer students' questions regarding resolving conflicts.
- After being trained in general mediation skills, students may be asked to implement a Peer Mediation type program to be used in their school; one that would be easy for students their age to understand.
- The students may be asked to keep a log of how they use conflict mediation, if the program is developed in their school. They may keep a journal of their experiences expressing how they felt during the mediation process.

Negate the Issue
"Rules for Mediation" Handout

When resolving conflicts certain ground rules should always be followed to allow working toward a successful resolution.

1. **Participation**: everyone is encouraged to participate

2. **Respect**: Everyone will respect one another's ideas and feelings.

3. **Support**: Everyone will support each other as they take risks to try out new skills and ideas.

4. **Confidentiality**: Everyone will respect outside of class what is said in class.

5. Everyone will remain **open and honest**.

6. **No name calling** will be allowed.

7. Everyone **speaks in turn**.

8. **No one should interrupt** when others are speaking.

Negate the Issue
"Styles of Conflict Resolution" Handout

Certain styles of conflict resolution are usually apparent in individuals. They may vary according to the situation but people have a tendency to favor one style.

1. **Avoidant behaviors**:   allows oneself to be interrupted, has poor eye contact, poor posture, withholds information, is an ineffective listener, indecisive, and often denies behavior.

2. **Problem-solving behavior**:   states feelings, has good eye contact, good posture, discloses information, is an effective listener, approaches with skill, and takes clear positions.

3. **Aggressive behaviors**:   interrupts, has glaring eye contact, displays arrogant air about him/herself, conceals information, dominates, and is loud, abusive, and blames others.

Negate the Issue
"Conflict Mediation Process" Handout

Stage I - Introduction

In this stage mediators:

1. Greet and shake hands with the disputants
2. Explain about confidentiality
3. Explain that disputants take turns talking about the problem
4. Explain about taking breaks if needed*
5. Explain the ground rules
6. Explain that a written agreement will be made between the disputants

Stage II - Storytelling

Mediators will:

1. Listen to each party's side of the story and then paraphrase facts and feelings back to the disputants.
2. Summarize whole story after each side has been clearly heard.
3. Note any common ground found between disputants.
4. Disputants will: State each other's point of view.

Stage III - Finding Solutions

1. Issues are named by the mediators and the disputants
2. Disputants brainstorm solutions
3. Ask disputants how they can agree.

Stage IV - Agreements

1. Disputants and mediators restate solutions
2. Agreement is written upon finding compromising solution. Agreement must be clear and concise; as specific as possible.
3. Congratulate disputants for coming to resolution.

* breaks are known as caucuses...and are usually done in later stages when disputants are not able to communicate about the situation. Disputants are each removed and taken aside, to talk to the mediators separately, then resume session often with mediators discussing aspects of the problem that are difficult for the disputants to discuss. This is all done under the disputant's consent.

Date_____

Dear Parent/Guardian:

In the activity "Negate the Issue" the students learned the process and steps for conflict mediation. They were taught the ground rules, the behavioral responses, as well as the actual stages in mediation development.

As a parent, your natural tendency may be to shield your child from conflict. Unfortunately, conflict is a part of life, and your child will be encountering difficult situations. With your continued help and support, he/she will learn to become more comfortable and more confident in dealing with conflicts. Learning the conflict mediation process may not only benefit your child at school, but also at work and other social settings.

Your child may interview family members to see various similarities and differences in dealing with conflict. You may wish to discuss how your family deals with conflicts. Is your family familiar with the process of conflict mediation? Discuss how your child and your family may obtain more information concerning mediation.

Sincerely,

_____

It's Amazing

Objectives

Students will:

✔ explore conflict resolution including the styles, steps and stages of mediation.

✔ learn team building skills

✔ examine perspectives on conflict

Materials Needed

"It's Amazing Maze" handout
"It's Amazing Questions"
Pencil
Scissors

Procedures

1. Make five or six copies of the "It's Amazing Maze" handout.

2. Cut each maze handout apart.

3. Divide the class into five or six groups.

4. Randomly choose a group to begin.

5. Ask the group to choose a section from the "It's Amazing Questions."

6. Ask the question from the section they chose, if the group answers correctly give them the piece of the maze.

7. Continue allowing each group to answer questions and collect pieces of the maze until a group has collected all the pieces.

8. Once the groups have collected all the pieces to the maze have them as a group, find their way through the maze. The first group to complete the maze is the winner.

Discussion Questions

1. What role does conflict play in your life?
2. What have you learned and how will you use it?
3. Can conflict be positive?
4. Does everyone experience conflict?
5. What is the value in knowing conflict resolution?
6. What is the earliest conflict in which you were involved and how did you deal with it?

Variations

- Instead of a maze on the pieces of paper, clues could be listed to a winners circle. Thus the students will look for the hidden treasure which is the winners circle.

- Use a haunted house and have "actors" play witches and ghosts who are having a conflict. Students must help these ghouls solve their conflict.

- Hold a murder mystery, each time a group answers a question, they are given a clue as to "who done it."

- Hold a mock mediation session, going through the various stages. Stop at each phase and ask each group a question. Upon answering the questions, the resolution process moves on to the next step in that stage. Each time a group answers a question correctly they earn a point. The team with the most points at the end is the winner.

It's Amazing
"Questions"

The correct answers to the questions listed below are located at the end of the question in parentheses.

Conflict Conclusion

1. Conflict always spells negativity. T or (F)
2. Everyone views conflict in a positive way at some point. T or (F)
3. With conflict resolution comes the opportunity for personal _____. (growth)
4. Conflicts allow individuals to come to agreements which may perhaps improve their situations in life. (T) or F
5. Conflict is an inevitable part of life. (T) or F

Getting the Big Picture

1. _____is what one sees from a given perspective. (Point of view)
2. People have different perspectives because they only know their own thoughts and feelings, not the other persons who is involved. (T) or F
3. Our bodies tell our emotions, even when our voices don't. (T) or F
4. Point of view can change. (T) or F
5. Each participant brings a point of view and emotions to mediation. (T) or F

Team Building

1. What is teamwork?
   a. Digging a ditch by yourself
   (b.) Working as a team to achieve a common goal
   c. All the work a team has to do

2. Depending on others means
   a. Trusting others to do their job
   (b.) Needing others to reach a goal
   c. Waiting for others

3. Which of the following would require team work?
   (a.) Building a house
   (b.) Flying to the moon
   c. Breathing

4. Tell of a time when you depended on others. (Accept all reasonable answers.)

5. Tell of a time when someone depended on you. (Accept all reasonable answers.)

168

It's Amazing

"Questions"

The correct answers to the questions listed below are located at the end of the question in parentheses.

Party Time

1. Listing possibilities is a step to problem solving. (T) or F
2. Making a choice is not a step to problem solving. T or (F)
3. Considering the consequences of your actions is the last step to problem solving. T or (F)
4. Reflecting means to think about your choice. (T) or F
5. Tell one way you are similar to another person in the group. (Accept all reasonable answers.)

Work it Out

1. The problem solving method is a useful tool in trying to resolve conflicts. (T) or F.
2. What is the last step in the problem solving process? (Reflect on choices)
3. There is only one best solution to every conflict. T or (F)
4. Problem solving is a continual skill we use in everyday life. (T) or F
5. It is always easier to work out solutions to conflicts with a partner. T or (F)

Wheel of Conflict

1. Paraphrasing is a skill we are born knowing how to do. T or (F).
2. The definition of paraphrasing is stating back thoughts, feelings, and_____ about a conflict that is being discussed. (facts)
3. Many people find paraphrasing difficult to master at first (T) or F
4. Each person paraphrases using the same words. T or (F)
5. The value in learning to paraphrase well is that it leads to greater understanding of the conflict. (T) or F

Negate the Issue

1. People always feel comfortable using conflict mediation as a way to resolve conflicts. T or (F)
2. Mediation is a skill that requires practice in order to become proficient. (T) or F
3. Which one of the following is not a ground rule to be used when discussing conflicts? Support, confidentiality, judging, respect   (judging)
4. Everyone is aware that conflict mediation exists as a mode to resolving problems. T or (F)
5. Once mediation is used, all problems permanently go away. T or (F).

It's Amazing
"Maze" Handout

This puzzle was created at www.puzzlemaker.com by Network Solutions Developers, Inc.

Date_____

Dear Parent/Guardian:

Today the students reviewed in "It's Amazing" the parts and process of conflict resolution. The students reviewed perspectives of conflict, how to build and make decisions as a team, they learned problem-solving techniques, how to paraphrase, and understand the mediation process.

As a parent you struggle to help your child when he/she is going through a conflict. By continually being supportive and practicing effective conflict resolution skills within your family, you are promoting the acquisition of a valuable life skill. Your child will deal with future conflicts armed with the knowledge, practice and confidence needed to resolve issues.

This may be applied at home when a conflict arises. Your child can help mediate if they are not involved in the conflict by having them make up role play situations between other siblings so skills can be practiced. Encouraging your child to use the process when conflicts arise will solidify the process in his/her mind and make its use second nature. Keep up the good work toward encouraging your child to resolve conflicts peacefully.

Sincerely,

_____

Chapter 6

Study Skills

"I am convinced that it is of primordial importance to learn more every year than the year before. After all, what is education but a process by which a person begins to learn how to learn?"

- Peter Ustinov

By using the study skills lesson, students strive to become independent, life-long learners. It is intended to help students improve in the following: awareness of learning styles, arranging work space for efficiency, memory with mnemonic devices, note taking, planning, organizing, and listening skills.

Lost in Space

Objectives

Students will:

✔ evaluate their study area for effectiveness

✔ learn how to improve study areas that are weak

Materials Needed

Paper

Pencil

"Study Area Evaluation Guide" handout

Procedures

1. Identify a "work area" for homework.

2. Ask the students to draw or describe the study area they have at home. If a student does not have one at home, have him/her draw or describe one he/she feels would be appropriate.

3. Allow the students to share.

4. Discuss the goal of a study area.

5. Discuss the following categories about a work area:

Auditory	What sounds are heard, how loud are those sounds, what effect does hearing those sounds have on studying
Visual	What can be seen, are the things which can be seen, moving or stationary
Study Area	Size, location (is it near a high traffic area), degree to which materials can be spread out
Seating	Is there a place for you to sit, what is that seat like: firmness, size, on wheels, accessibility of study area from chair
Supply Accessibility	Are frequently used items easily accessible (i.e. pencil, paper), how are frequently used items stored, what materials are in study area which do not belong there.

6. Choose a study area in the room or school or use a picture of one. As a class, use the "Study Area Evaluation Guide" handout to evaluate the work area for effectiveness.

7. Put the students in groups and have them list the changes they would make to the area to improve its effectiveness. Let them discuss the results of the "Study Area Evaluation Guide." Have them put a star beside the questions that resulted in answers they would like to change. Have them put a circle around the improvements, which they could not make themselves, but would need adult assistance to improve.

8. Discuss the improvements needed.

9. Ask the students to take out the pictures or descriptions of their home study area.

10. Have the students use the same guide to evaluate this area.

11. Have them list the changes they would make to the area to improve its effectiveness. Once again, ask them to circle the improvements, which would require adult assistance to improve.

Discussion Questions

1. What did you learn about study areas? Yours?
2. Does it matter if a study area is effective? Why?
3. Can we control the effectiveness of a study area? How?
4. How did you feel about the results of the effectiveness of your home study area?
5. Do individual differences effect the efficiency of the home study area? How?

Variations

• The student could be sent home with the evaluation to evaluate their study area instead of doing it from their picture or description.
• Students could be sent home with a partner to evaluate one another's study area.
• Students may create an efficient study area by using catalogs to pick out or eliminate items to be included in the study area.
• Have the students develop their own list of aspects needed for an efficient work area. Present these ideas to the class and have a "speak out" on how they feel about these aspects to help them improve their own study areas.

Lost in Space?

"Study Area Evaluation Guide" Handout

Before filling out the rest of this guide, how do you feel about your study area right now?

_____ Great, needs no improvement
_____ Needs some improvement
_____ Needs minor improvement
_____ Needs major improvement

Sounds

1. How many sounds do you hear?
    _____ Many   _____ Some   _____ Few   _____ None

2. How loud are the sounds you hear?
    _____ Very loud   _____ Medium loud _____ Slight volume _____ No sound

3. How distracting to you are the sounds you hear?
    _____ Very   _____ Some   _____ Minor   _____ None

Visual

4. How many things do you see in your study area other than your work?
    _____ Many   _____ Some   _____ Few   _____ None

5. Are the things you see moving or stationary?
    _____ Most are moving
    _____ Some are moving
    _____ A few are moving
    _____ None are moving

6. How distracting to you are the moving things?
    _____ Very   _____ Some   _____ Few   _____ None

7. How is the lighting in your study area?
    _____ Too bright   _____ Bright   _____ Dim   _____ Too dim

Work Space

8. How is the location of the work space?
    _____ Great, needs no improvement
    _____ Needs some improvement
    _____ Needs minor improvement
    _____ Needs major improvement

9. How is the amount of space?
    _____ Great, needs no improvement
    _____ Needs some improvement
    _____ Needs minor improvement
    _____ Needs major improvement

Supplies

10. How accessible are regularly used supplies? (i.e. pencil, paper, etc.)
    _____ Very   _____ Some   _____ A little   _____ Not at all

11. How many unnecessary items are located in the study area?
    _____ Very   _____ Some   _____ Few   _____ None

Seating

12. Is there a place for you to sit in your study area?
    _____ Yes   _____ Sometimes   _____ No

13. How comfortable is the place in which you sit?
    _____ Very   _____ Some   _____ A little   _____ Not at all

14. How accessible is the work area from your seat?
    _____ Very   _____ Some   _____ A little   _____ Not at all

After filling out this guide, how do you feel about your study area?
_____ Great, needs no improvement
_____ Needs some improvement
_____ Needs minor improvement
_____ Needs major improvement

Date_____

Dear Parent/Guardian:

Today in the activity, "Lost in Space?", we discussed the qualities of a study area including visual, auditory, work space, seating and supply accessibility. The students ranked study areas including the one they have at home. The ranking was based on effectiveness. They also discussed how to enhance work areas with their peers.

Grades four through eight are often a confusing and changing time for students. During the many changes they are going through, your support, patience, and encouragement can help them glide through the process. Learning organization skills at this time will be a much needed skill used throughout life. Developing effective work areas can help them achieve their goals, by speeding up the overall organization process.

Please ask your child to share the ranking of his/her home study area. During the activity, they made an improvement plan for their home study area. On this improvement plan they circled the areas with which they would need adult assistance to change. You may wish to help your child make some or all of the suggested changes. Your child may also need to discuss the study area and the affect he/she feels it has on him/her. Further discussion may be done on the over all importance of studying to the family.

Sincerely,

_____

Putting It All Together

Objectives

Students will:

✔ define organization

✔ examine ways to become more organized

Materials Needed

Two pencils

Notebook or paper where homework is listed

Book bags

Procedures

1. Define what organization means with the class.

2. Ask the students to take out their homework.

3. Give them three to four minutes of time to organize their homework.

4. Have the students take out two pencils. See which student takes out the pencils the quickest.

5. Ask them to take a piece of notebook paper. See who brings out the paper the fastest.

7. Put each student who produced the articles the fastest, into groups with others students who had a more difficult time getting organized. Have those students who were the fastest, explain to their group his/her way of getting organized.

8. Give all group members time to reorganize their homework assignments after they have learned some of these new methods.

9. Discuss as a class which methods were the most effective helping students become more organized.

Discussion Questions

1. How organized did you feel you already were before beginning this activity?
2. What new methods did you learn that will now help you become more organized?
3. How important is it to be organized in school and with your assignments?
4. Does everyone use the same methods for getting organized? Which methods were used the most? The least?
5. How can you now teach a peer to become organized with his/her book bag?
6. How can you detect when a student is disorganized and may need help?

Variations

• If the students do not carry book bags or a binder, they may use their lockers to store assignments. They may be placed into teams whereupon they see who can organize their lockers the fastest. Or they may do this with partners.

• For classrooms that have desks with spaces to place books, pencils, etc., students can learn how to organize their own personal desks.

• Teachers and counselors can hold weekly contests where they check to see who is the most organized. Awards can be given to those students who are the most organized. Then those students can become monitors for other students by taking the rest of that week and checking their peers' book bags for organization at the end of the day.

• School-wide contests in homerooms can be held where teachers/counselors check to see who is the most organized. Contests can be held where the students with the most organization can be rewarded.

Date_____

Dear Parent/Guardian:

"Putting It All Together" is what organization means. Organization is an important part of everyday life. The students examined ways to become more organized by seeing who was able to bring out their homework the fastest.

During grades four through eight, this is a crucial time for your child to learn how to gather homework assignments and to keep them organized. Encourage your child to seek help to improve their organizational skills by seeing their school counselor or teacher. Continue to show your child praise as he/she becomes more organized with time.

At home, discuss what organization exists in the family lifestyle. What role does organization play? Assign your child a task to organize such as a short family trip, family reunion, or event. Discuss how they could make changes to the event to become even more organized if needed.

Sincerely,

_____

Perfect Timing

Objectives

Students will:

✔ learn to use planning time to improve effectiveness

✔ learn to use a schedule to plan homework and daily assignments

Materials Needed

Two pictures
Pen
Watch or timer
"Schedule" handout

Procedures

Set Up: Make one copy of each picture per team. Fold the picture in half horizontally two times, making three crease marks. Fold the pictures in half vertically two times, making three crease marks. To make the pictures more difficult for older students, fold them in half three times both horizontally and vertically to make seven crease marks in each direction. Cut the pictures into pieces by cutting on the crease marks. Put the pieces of one picture in an envelope. Cut the second picture pieces the same size as the first by following the same procedure described above. For each team be sure to prepare the picture pieces of the same size for each picture.

1. Divide the class into 4-5 teams.

2. Pass out a copy of the same picture to each team.

3. Give the teams a few minutes to put the picture together.

4. Explain to the students that they are going to put together another picture with a difficulty level similar to the first one.

5. Give the teams two minutes to plan how they are going to put together the next picture.

6. Now pass out the next picture.

7. Have the teams then figure out what the image is in the picture.

8. As a class, have the teams discuss how they put the picture together.

9. Hold a discussion on how planning affected how they pieced the picture together.

10. Pass out the "Schedule" handout. Explain this is how they can make a schedule to better manage their time.

11. Ask them to go home and develop their own time management schedule.

12. Have the students include in their schedule homework, chores from home, and time for fun activities. They may also include bedtimes, dinner times, and any long range chores or assignments.

Discussion Questions

1. How did planning out ahead of time effect your solving the puzzle?
2. Did planning make it easier for you to solve the puzzle? If so, how?
3. How important is it to learn to manage your time when studying?
4. How can what you learned today be applied to managing your time when you are actually studying?
5. Is time management a natural and easy skill to learn?
6. How can learning time management skills affect your grades?

Variations

- Besides pictures, crafts can be brought in or developed. Allow the students time to plan how they will make the crafts.
- Students can keep diaries of their schedules for a few days and then bring them into class. They may discuss these diaries and see how their peers managed their time. This may give them additional ideas as to how to improve or manage their own schedules especially for homework assignments.
- Students may be asked to develop their own time management checklist that they can share with the class.
- The students may be given buddies whereupon they check with each other daily to see methods of how they manage their time. They can give each other ideas on how to improve and make more planning time concerning homework and solving problems.
- Teams can also teach other teams the methods they chose when piecing together the pictures.
- Bring in two puzzles from home instead of the pictures previously used.

Perfect Timing

"Schedule" Handout

Time	Monday	Tuesday	Wednesday	Thursday	Friday
4:00 - 4:30					
4:30 - 5:00					
5:00 - 5:30					
5:30 - 6:00					
6:00 - 6:30					
6:30 - 7:00					
7:00 - 7:30					
7:30 - 8:00					
8:00 - 8:30					
8:30 - 9:00					
9:00 - 9:30					
9:30 - 10:00					
10:00 - 10:30					
10:30 - 11:00					

Date_____

Dear Parent/Guardian:

Today in the activity "Perfect Timing" the students examined ways to manage their time in completing puzzles. They learned how to apply these methods toward getting their school work completed. They also learned how to develop schedules to follow daily to help them manage their time more effectively.

Your child at this age, may tend to have a hard time getting assignments completed in a timely manner. This is not unusual, and with your continual support, your child can learn methods to improve time management skills. Many of the methods just require consistency, patience, and practice.

At home you may choose to look at how your child manages his/her time in completing homework. You may also choose to see if similar patterns are occurring between other siblings. Ask your child how he/she can make improvements in time management during school and with chores at home. Allow opportunities for your child to practice accomplishing certain tasks in a designated time period. Reward your child when he/she has successfully mastered the task in the given time frame.

Sincerely,

_____

Hear, See, Do

Objective
Students will:
✔ experience and evaluate different styles of learning to find their personal learning preference

Materials Needed
Several pieces of paper
Directions on how to make three origami objects

Procedures

Set up: a. Put the directions for "Origami A" in learning area "A."

          b. Record verbal directions or have an individual read directions for "Origami B" in learning area "B."

          c. Use the directions "Origami C" to assemble the remaining origami object. Leave this assembled object as an example of the finished product for students to examine and manipulate in learning area "C."

1. Discuss with the students that learning may take place by an auditory method, visually, or kinesthetically. Explain what each of these ways of learning means.

2. Put the students in pairs and have them discuss what things they like to do and how they think they learn best.

3. Put the students into three groups.

4. Send each group to one of the learning areas. Give them time to complete the task.

5. Have each group rotate to a different learning area.

6. Continue until each group has experienced each of the learning centers.

7. Discuss and have the students decide which learning preference they have.

Discussion Questions

1. For which learning style did you have a preference?
2. How strong of a preference did you have for your desired learning style?
3. Was there a learning style that was particularly weak?
4. What have you learned about your way of learning and how will you use it?
5. Is it important to know your learning style? Why?
6. Are certain learning styles more effective with certain subject areas than other styles?
7. Which style for which subject?
8. Would it be helpful to combine learning styles? If so, how and why?

Variations

- Start with an informal evaluation of the students current classes and why they learn more or less easily in each of those classes.
- Set a goal for students and closely monitor how they obtain that goal. Ask them why they chose the method(s) they did.
- Have students brainstorm a list of ways to accomplish a goal. Allow them to choose their method.

Hear, See, Do
"Origami A"

To be left in learning area "A"

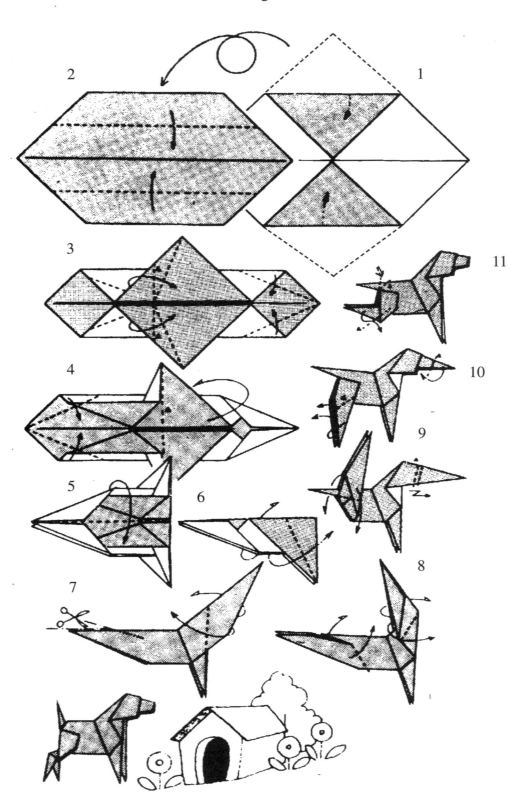

Hear, See, Do

"Origami B"

To be left in learning area "B"

1. Use a square piece of paper.

2. Fold down paper diagonally from one corner to another (so you have a crease).

3. Unfold.

4. Fold paper diagonally in opposite direction (so it has two creases that form an x).

5. Unfold.

6. Take each corner and fold down to the center of the "x." The paper should not overlap.

7. Flip paper over and fold each corner into the center again. The paper should not over-lap.

8. Flip paper over.

9. Fold side of paper with squares in half, unfold, then fold it in half the opposite way.

10. Unfold.

11. Take right thumb and place it under square flap. Place right index finger under square flap to the right of the flap under which the right thumb is resting.

12. Take left thumb and place it under square flap that is beside where the right thumb is resting.

13. Put left index finger under remaining square flap.

14. Pinch fingers together.

Hear, See, Do
"Origami C"

To be left in learning area "C"

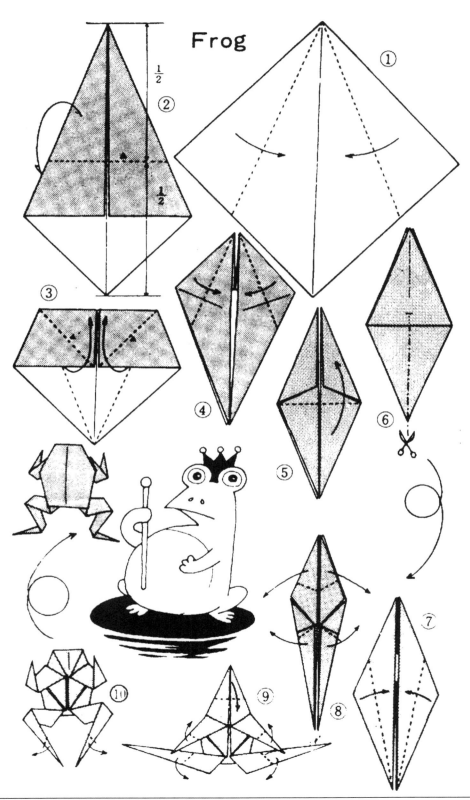

Frog

Date_____

Dear Parent/Guardian:

The students learned about their preference for learning styles with the activity "Hear, See, Do." We experienced learning by visual, auditory, and kinesthetic (hands-on) methods. Being aware of your learning style may help enhance learning, increase acquisition of knowledge, and therefore improve the quality of life.

As a parent, by understanding your child's style of learning, you can provide the greatest support and educational resources to him/her to achieve success academically. By your child learning to comprehend new information through his/her "preferred" learning style, may lead to greater knowledge, acquisition and increased self-confidence.

Since you were your child's first teacher, you may wish to continue helping your child learn. It is important for your child to use all of his/her senses and not just rely on his/her "preferred style" in certain situations. For instance, ask your child what senses would be used if there was a power outage. Encourage your child to strengthen his/her auditory sense by giving only verbal directions. You may also wish to have your child learn a procedure simply from a model with no auditory input given.

Sincerely,

_____

Picture This

Objective

Students will:

✔ learn to listen to directions

Materials Needed

Pencils
Paper
Markers
Tape
"Object for Drawing" sheet

Procedures

1. Discuss with class that they will be learning to improve and perfect their listening skills.

2. Group the students into pairs.

3. Have the partners sit in chairs facing the same way, less than an arm's length away from each other.

4. Have the person in the rear, tape a piece of construction paper on the front person's back.

5. While you are looking at the "Objects for Drawing" sheet, give exact directions on how to draw the picture. Do not name the object.

7. The person in the rear will draw the object as directions are given and their partner will visualize the object.

8. Have the students that visualized name what object they think should have been drawn on the paper taped to their back. Have the person who drew the object, remove it and show it to their partner and the class.

9. Have the students switch roles and repeat steps 7 and 8.

10. Have class discuss how accurate the drawings were by the directions given.

Discussion Questions

1. How easy or difficult was it for you to draw the object while listening to the directions?
2. For the person whose back was being drawn on, could you tell what the object was going to be?
3. How did it feel being able to follow directions purely by using listening skills only?
4. How important is it for us to improve our listening skills? What methods can be used to improve our skills?
5. On a scale of one to ten with ten being the greatest, where would you place your level of effective listening skills?

Variations

- Instead of one person giving directions to everyone. Give one partner in each pair the picture and allow them to give directions to their partner. This will allow the students to experience verbalizing directions and receiving them. To do this, partners will need to have their backs to one another.
- Have the students write directions to a simple, everyday event (i.e. sharpening a pencil). Then pair students up and have them read their directions to their partner. The partner must follow the directions completely without questioning. See how accurate the directions were.
- Play a round of "Simon Says." Discuss the listening skill involved.
- Clap a rhythm. Have the students listen and repeat it.

Picture This
"Object for Drawing" Sheet

Date_____

Dear Parent/Guardian:

In the activity "Picture This" the students had to listen to and follow the directions given in order to draw the picture described.

Listening is a skill that is used several times daily. Listening can help us be better students or better friends.

As a parent you have eagerly listened to your child's wants and needs. You can now help your child learn to listen. Discuss how your family listens and the times in which listening is important to your family. You may make a game out of following directions. Hide a small prize and give directions to locate it!

Sincerely,

_____

Take Notice

Objective

Students will:

✔ learn the steps to note taking from an auditory source of information

Materials Needed

Pen or pencil
Paper
Information to be presented
"Note Taking Tips" handout

Procedures

1. Explain to the students that they are to take notes about information that will be presented by an auditory method.

2. Give students paper and a pen or pencil.

3. Read the information or play information from a prerecorded source.

4. Have the students take notes.

5. In small groups, allow the students to share the notes they have taken.

6. Have them discuss the methods or ideas for taking notes, which they found to be positive.

7. Pass out the "Note Taking Tips" handout and review it.

8. Give the students information again in an auditory manner and have them take notes using the tips discussed.

Discussion Questions

1. How important is note taking?
2. Has this activity changed the way in which you take notes and if so, how?
3. What would be necessary in order for this information to be more helpful?
4. If you were already using these Note Taking Tips prior to the lesson, can you think of any other ways to improve your skills?
5. How could you develop a note taking strategy that you could teach to your peers?

Variations

- In the same lesson, introduce mapping and outlining as ways of taking notes from written material.
- Allow a student to tell a partner about the events of the day and the partner will take notes on what is said. Partners will switch roles.
- Have two people jointly interview a third person and take notes. Allow students to compare notes and the organization of the notes as well as the main idea(s) said by the speaker.
- Have the students read an informational article and highlight the important information.

Take Notice
"Note Taking Tips" Handout

1. Be an active listener by doing the following.

   Restate   Put what the speaker has said in your own words.
   Summarize   Repeat the major ideas, themes and feelings expressed.
   Clarify   Ask questions to be sure of what the speaker said.

2. Picture it - try to create a "picture" in your mind about what is being said.

3. Choose a method for taking notes. Think about how the speaker has organized the material. There may be a written outline or he/she may be using a class discussion.

4. Use only words or phrases not complete sentences. Write down the main ideas.

5. When you are told you need to know something be sure to write it down. This is a hint that it is important.

Remember your notes are for you. Make sure you can read them clearly and easily. Do not worry about anyone else's opinions regarding the notes.

Date_____

Dear Parent/Guardian:

In "Taking Notes", our activity for today, we wanted the students to learn to take detailed notes. The students learned strategies for taking notes when information was spoken. They practiced using these strategies.

Listening is an important skill that will help students achieve their full potential. Listening is more than just hearing. It is organizing information in writing so that it can be easily understood and used at a later time. Note taking is a life long skill that will be used frequently.

As a parent, you want to see your child to do the best he/she can. At home, teach the whole family the listening strategies. The family could practice while members of the family tell about what happened to them that day. The telephone can be an exciting matching tool that can be used to encourage note taking. Teach your child to take notes, then let him/her practice by recording phone messages in writing.

Sincerely,

_____

Unforgettable

Objectives

Students will:

✔ learn the steps to one method of improving memory

✔ practice increasing memory using one method

Materials Needed

Pen or pencil
"Strategies for Improving Memory" handout

Procedures

Set up: Prearrange with someone to have them come into the class immediately after you give the students their paper and pen or pencil. Ask this person to walk around in a complete circle and then leave, taking approximately one minute for the whole process.

1. Give the students a pen or pencil and paper.

2. Have the prearranged visitor enter the class at this point.

3. Have students write down everything they can remember about the person, including all physical characteristics and details about clothing being worn or objects being held by the individual.

4. Allow the students to share their notes with the class.

5. Have the person return to the room and remain for a few minutes, giving students an opportunity to check their notes for accuracy.

6. Have students who had high numbers of accuracies to describe any strategies they employed.

7. Pass out the "Strategies for Improving Memory" handout and discuss it.

8. Practice using the strategies with some of the following words. As the word is given, have the students sketch a picture to help them remember the definition of the word.

Sambar   deer with pointed antlers
Olfactory pertaining to the sense of smell
Peruke   a wig
Imagery   mental picture
Wobble   to move unsteadily from side to side
Monsoon   a periodic wind
Deuce   two

9. Have the students share their sketches with the class and discuss.

Discussion Questions

1. Is memory important? Why?
2. In what ways do you most rely on memory?
3. What was the most difficult step in learning this way of improving memory?
4. What was easiest about the procedure for remembering?
5. What have you learned and when will you use it?

Variations

- Use the methods for improving memory that you learned in this lesson in other subject areas, such as learning capitals and states, multiplication tables and spelling words.
- The students could compose individual dictionaries using their sketches of the words.
- Have the students dramatize words in addition to sketching them.
- Allow the students to teach the strategies for improving memory to a group of younger students.

Unforgettable
"Strategies for Improving Memory" Handout

OAR can be used to help improve memory.

O bserved

A ssociated

R emembered

When we associate or relate a word to something familiar or memorable, we truly observe it or take note of it, thus resulting in remembering it.

To remember the meaning of a word think of something that sounds like the word. Then create a visualization of that word. Make this visualization unique or colorful so it sticks out in your mind.

For example, rotund, which is an adjective meaning plump; rounded.
Rho ton sounds like the word. I visualize a female named Rho, short for Rhoda, who is round and is sitting on a scale that registers a ton, thus she is plump and round.

Try rabies as another example. Rabies - an acute, infectious, viral disease of the central nervous system, often fatal which is transmitted by the bite of an infected animal. Ray bees sounds like the word. I visualize a ray, or line protruding from a point. This ray is made up of rabid bees, which can infect with a sting.

Date_____

Dear Parent/Guardian:

Today's lesson, "Unforgettable", presented a colorful way to help students improve memory. Students were given unfamiliar words and their definitions. They thought of something that sounded like the word. They then created a visualization of the word. The visualization should be as creative and memorable as possible.

Throughout life students will be expected to remember everything from capitals to multiplication facts. Making it fun can lighten what can be a heavy load.

Your child has provided you with many memories you will treasure for years to come. You can help him/her improve his/her memory for useful daily needs. You may have your child practice using memory skills by memorizing the grocery list or the "to do" list. Another fun game to improve memory is to memorize things seen as you travel together. For instance, ask your child to remember the last three streets you passed or the color of the last four cars that passed. Memory gets better with practice, so make it fun and include as many senses as possible. Enjoy!

Sincerely,

_____

Bursting with Study Skills

Objective

Students will:

✔ review the components and application of study skills

Materials Needed

Seven different colors of balloons
(five balloons of each color for a total
of thirty-five balloons)
"Bursting with Study Skills Questions"
Paper
Seven different colored markers
(the seven colors need to be the same as the
seven colors of the balloons)

Procedures

Set up: a. Separate the questions

b. Put one question inside each balloon and blow up the balloon. *Note* All the questions from the same lesson should be put into separate balloons of the same
color. For instance, all the questions from lesson two will be put in blue balloons
and the questions from lesson one put in red balloons.

1. Put the students in groups and have them name their group.

2. Give each group one sheet of paper and ask them to put their name on the sheet.

3. Have one team select a balloon, burst the balloon by sitting on it. The student that burst
the balloon will read the question out loud and then along with the other team members will answer the question.

4. If the question is answered correctly put a mark the same color as the balloon on that
team's sheet of paper. If the question was not answered correctly, do not put any marks.
It is another teams' turn.

5. Repeat steps 3 and 4 until each team has had a turn.

6. Teams who have answered their questions correctly will choose a balloon that is a different color from the one they previously burst. If they did not answer the question correctly, they may not choose another color balloon.

7. The goal of the game is to be the first team to get a mark of each color.

Discussion Questions

1. What color of balloon was most difficult for your team to obtain?
2. What did you learn and how will you use it?
3. Are study skills a natural part of the learning process?
4. Does having study skills benefit you and if so, how?
5. What are the different times in which you could apply these study skills?
6. Which study skill is the most important and why?

Variations

• Instead of using balloons, use paper airplanes. Use tape to place eight marks on the floor approximately eighteen inches apart. Label each area between the marks with a number between one and seven. Have the students throw a paper airplane and answer a question from which ever area the tip of the plane lands. Students need to answer questions from each of the areas. The student who answers the most questions wins.

• Rather than putting the questions in balloons the questions could be placed in bags (a separate one for each lesson). Students could draw out questions and answer them.

• Assign each question a number and have students pick a number and answer the question that corresponds to the number chosen.

• Assign a color for each question from a lesson. Use a multi-colored spinner, students will answer a question that corresponds to the color spun.

Bursting with Study Skills
"Questions"

The correct answers to the questions listed below are located at the end of the question in parentheses. There is also an answer key located on page 208 that may be cut apart and used for the balloons.

Lost in Space

1. All work spaces are ample in size. T or (F)
2. Lighting is an important consideration when planning a study area. (T) or F
3. The seat in a study area can never be too comfortable. T or (F)
4. A work area can have too many things in it. (T) or F
5. Which of the following should not be considered when evaluating a study area?
   a. Sounds
   b. What can be seen
   (c.) How the area would affect someone else if they were to use it.
   d. Supply accessibility

Putting It All Together

1. It is important to always be organized for class. T or (F)
2. Organization comes naturally to everyone. T or (F)
3. Being organized means being able to easily find your assignment. (T) or F
4. Organization is a skill that can be learned. (T) or F
5. Everyone wants to be organized. (T) or F

Perfect Timing

1. Learning to manage your time can improve your grades. (T) or F
2. Your peers and friends can teach you better ways to use your time. (T) or F
3. Everyone uses the same method when trying to plan an activity or event. T or (F)
4. Time management skills can increase your level for overall success. (T) or F
5. Time management can be helpful in planning a long range project. (T) or F

Hear, See, Do

1. Each person has a preferred learning style. (T) or F
2. Learning can take place auditorially, visually, or kinesthetically. (T) or F
3. Kinesthetic learning involves learning by touching or doing. (T) or F
4. Auditory learning involves learning by seeing T or (F)
5. Visual learning involves learning by hearing. T or (F)

Bursting with Study Skills
"Questions"

The correct answers to the questions listed below are located at the end of the question in parentheses. There is also an answer key located on page 208 that may be cut apart and used for the balloons.

Picture This

1. Having to listen to direction in order to learn is an example of the _____ style of learning. (auditory)
2. People retain information most frequently by auditory means. T or (F)
3. What we don't understand through hearing, we may pick up through seeing. (T) or F
4. It is always easy to hear everything and understand the teacher. T or (F)
5. Everyone interprets directions in the same way. T or (F)

Take Notice

1. When listening, one should try to connect new information to what is already known. (T) or F
2. You should always use complete sentences when taking notes. T or (F)
3. It is not important to write down something if your teacher tells you that you need to know it. T or (F)
4. It is a good idea to be aware of how the speaker has organized the information. (T) or F
5. When taking notes, do not picture what is being said. Picturing it will only distract you. T or (F)

Unforgettable

1. It is important to observe something in order to remember it. (T) or F
2. It is not necessary to associate new information to information we know in order to learn it. T or (F)
3. Associate means to relate something to what is already known. (T) or F
4. Making the association memorable will help solidify it in our minds. (T) or F
5. We cannot improve our memory. T or (F)

Bursting with Study Skills
"Questions" Answer Key for Balloons

Lost In Space	Hear, See, Do	Unforgettable
1. False	1. True	1. True
2. True	2. True	2. False
3. False	3. True	3. True
4. True	4. False	4. True
5. c	5. False	5. False

Putting It All Together	Picture This	
1. False	1. Auditory	
2. False	2. False	
3. True	3. True	
4. True	4. False	
5. True	5. False	

Perfect Timing	Take Notice	
1. True	1. True	
2. True	2. False	
3. False	3. False	
4. True	4. True	
5. True	5. False	

Date_____

Dear Parent/Guardian:

Today the students reviewed the study skills lessons by bursting balloons and answering questions found inside. The students earned a different color mark each time they answered a question from a different lesson. The goal was to answer a question from each lesson and obtain seven different color marks.

At home, you can encourage your child to use study skills when doing homework or when seeking information regarding a topic of personal interest. Study skills are also important life survival skills. Practicing study skills will help your child to improve him/herself in all areas.

Sincerely,

_____

Chapter 7

Positive Character Traits

"I cannot imagine how anyone can say, 'I'm weak' and then remain so.
After all, if you know it, why not fight against it,
why not try to train your character?"
- Anne Frank

The goal of this unit on positive character traits is to help the growing adolescent understand independent, different, and positive character within each student. The focus is on both internalization of individual traits in order to motivate the formation of goal setting and attitude toward success currently and in the future!

Character and the Affects on Me

Objective	Materials Needed
Students will: ✔ learn to identify positive character traits necessary for success and transfer these traits to his/her individual lives.	"Interview Outline" handout "Character and Me" handout

Procedures

Set up: a. One week prior to doing this activity discuss "Life Success." For example, students may see life success as professional accomplishments, monetary success, family, inner peacefulness, etc.

b. Students will be asked to think of a family member or friend whom they see as a successful adult.

c. Using the following interview outline, the student will be asked to call or write the person asking them to complete the interview sheet.

1. When interview sheets are brought to class, the "Character and Me" worksheet will be completed by each student.

2. The leader will facilitate a class discussion of the results of positive character traits found in each person interviewed.

3. An essay will then be assigned to each student to express their thoughts on "Character and the Effects on Me."

Discussion Questions

1. Reviewing the answers by the person interviewed, how could his/her life differ if other character choices were made (negative versus positive)?
2. When did this person begin making correct character choices (i.e., as a child, middle school student, etc.)?
3. How do your character choices affect you now? How will these affect your future?
4. How will your character choices affect those around you – family, friends, etc.?

Variations

- Combine with career lessons / goal setting to have students formulate a plan on how to implement good character choices even when faced with difficult situations in obtaining their goals.
- Discuss reputation versus character choices.
- Discuss the concept of blame rather than accepting the consequences of one's own choices.

Character and the Affects on Me!
"Interview Outline" Handout

Name: _____

Address: _____

Telephone: _____

Age: _____ Occupation: _____

Education: _____

1. How did you choose your current occupation? _____
_____
_____
_____

2. We have been studying good character traits, such as honesty, respect, responsibility, courage, kindness, etc. Which of these do you consider most important in your job and adult life? Why? _____
_____
_____
_____

3. Who taught you about good character? Have you always seen the importance of good character? If not, when did this become an important issue or part of your life?
_____
_____
_____

4. Since, currently, I am a middle school student, what advice can you offer me concerning my own character as I set future goals for my life? _____
_____
_____
_____

Miscellaneous discussion and comments with interview: _____
_____
_____

Character and the Affects on Me!
"Character and Me" Handout

1. What do I consider the most important part of the interview I conducted? Explain?

_____

_____

_____

2. Which good character traits do I think the person interviewed uses on a daily basis? Explain _____

_____

_____

_____

3. How can good character traits help me now? Why?

_____

_____

_____

4. Will my character and reputation in middle school affect my high school career? Will my high school years affect my young adult life? What part does my character play in this?

_____

_____

_____

5. What have I learned from this interview? Explain the affects of this interview on my life today and tomorrow. _____

_____

_____

Date_____

Dear Parent/Guardian:

Our students studied an extensive lesson on "Character and the Effects of Me!" today in class. The concentration was on positive character traits which are necessary for success now and in his/her future!

Your help is needed by discussing this lesson and what it means to your child. For example, "life success" in the areas of self, peaceful feelings within oneself, family, and accomplishments of all kinds were discussed. Students thought of adult(s) who are role models of success.

Essays have been assigned to express these individual thoughts on paper! I encourage you to review the essay with your child and encourage the positive character traits such as responsibility, respectfulness, honesty, etc.!

Choices are here for every one of us -- young and old ! How wonderful it will be if you, as the parent(s) with the assistance of the school, can teach our students positive character at this young age!

Sincerely,

_____

Courage for My Future

Objective

Students will:

✔ identify and begin to formulate areas in his/her own life that may need courageous actions to achieve goals

Materials Needed

"Courage Chart" handout
Notebook paper

Procedures

1. Define courage.

2. In chart form on a piece of notebook paper, students will "brainstorm" areas in their past, present, and future where courage "was", "is" and "might be" needed. (The leader may have sheets run off with this chart already arranged or the students can make their own charts.)

3. Have the class discuss and identify the common elements between students.

4. The leader will then assign students the task of identifying one role model (personal choice or famous person that has been read about) to write two paragraphs on "why" and "how" this person handled themselves courageously.

5. Finally, a creative essay will be assigned so that the student will "dream" about his/her future and talk about the courage that might be needed to achieve some personal goal(s).

Discussion Questions

1. Are there times when you should "step away" from a situation as a way to show your courage? Give an example.
2. Can you name visible ways that courage is shown to others?
3. What are some ways you "communicate" courage to others?
4. If you have ever experienced overwhelming fear, what form of courage did you use to overcome it?

Variations

- The leader will assign a literary work for students to review (such as *The Red Badge of Courage*, etc.) as an entire project on courage.
- Research heroes through literature stories or books in the school library and have students share orally with the class some of their findings.
- Discuss the armed forces of the United States and the courage that has been needed in the past (and the present) while defending our country.

Courage for My Future
"Courage Chart" Handout

My Courage of the PAST	My Courage in the PRESENT	Courage I May Need in the FUTURE

Date_____

Dear Parent/Guardian:

Today our students have been discussing "Courage for My Future!" It is never too early in life to set goals and realize the courage it takes to reach these goals!

Role models have been discussed and identified from either the student's personal choice or a famous person who has been read about through literature stories and/or books. The "why" and "how" of courage utilized by this person has been examined by your child.

At home, it would be beneficial to review the times courage is shown to others and the times that one must "step away" from situations (which also exhibits courage). If there are times your child is frightened (brief panic attacks), he/she may be willing to discuss this with you much more than he/she was willing to discuss in class today. Help identify the ways courageous thoughts or actions can help the next time this fear resurfaces!

Thank you for building character in your child and supporting our efforts from the school. Remember -- building character is building life skills that will broaden and enlighten your child's entire life span!

Sincerely,

_____

Respect for Self

Objective

Students will:

✔ directly correlate respect for self with current and future success

Materials Needed

Notebook paper

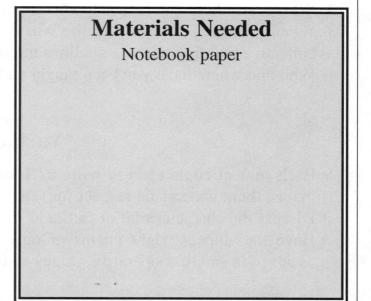

Procedures

1. Each student will brainstorm and list 3 good personality qualities about him/herself.

2. Using these good personality qualities, the student will write how these can benefit him/her now and in the future.

3. The leader could take these papers and list the good personality qualities from the students (without names, of course) and either write on the board or give a copy to each student.

4. Then the class members could be challenged to consider other qualities each might or might not possess and begin to build their good character traits in order to respect themselves more.

Discussion Questions

1. How do the qualities you listed help you the most?
2. Where will these qualities help you the most? Why?
3. When (at what point) in your life will these qualities be the most beneficial – or is a collective building of these qualities throughout your life span? Explain.
4. Who and where have you been taught and modeled respect?

Variations

- Each student could elect to write a "Thank You" to the person or persons who have helped them understand respect for self.
- Discuss the character trait of "attitude" in relationship to respect for self.
- Have the students right poems or raps concerning respect for self. This could be assigned in small, cooperative groups and performed for the class or younger children.

Date_____

Dear Parent/Guardian:

In learning about the character trait of RESPECT, our students' focus is on "Respect for Self!" In our lesson today, each student thought of at least 3 good personality qualities about him/herself. As these were discussed, each class member was challenged to consider other qualities each may or may not possess and begin to build their good character traits through habitual use, in order to respect him/herself more.

Respect for self is necessary as one builds goals and makes individual future plans! As the parent, you have helped to reinforce respect in your child prior to his/her school years. Now, as your child has reached an important (and, sometimes difficult) age, the school is attempting to reinforce that each of us is different and worthy of respecting our own positive character!

Thank you for helping to reinforce this at home!

Sincerely,

_____

Responsibility Reaction

Objective

Students will:

✔ internalize individual responsibilities and will react to these without being reminded

Materials Needed

"Sentence Starters" handout

Procedures

1. Two teams within the classroom will be named.

2. As this "Reaction" game begins, each student should have a pencil and paper handy to jot down personal thoughts as the sentences are completed orally. The leader may want to do the same on the board.

3. As the game begins, one student will choose a sentence starter on responsibility from a basket (or hat). The student will have 10 seconds to begin a verbal response. If unable to do so, the other team gets a point. If done successfully, his/her team gets the point.

4. At the completion of the game, points will be tallied and the winning team will be awarded an incentive (chosen by the leader) such as a free homework pass, etc.

Discussion Questions

1. Which responsibilities are the most difficult for you? Which are the easiest to remember and react to for you?

2. Do you feel it is easier to handle your responsibilities now than when you were younger? Why or why not?

3. Who are some adults that you admire for handling their responsibilities well? Why?

Variations

- The leader could give each team an equal number of sentence starters and have the teams design a bulletin board (or art project) using the ideas generated from the "reactions" to the sentences.
- Have the students explain a responsibility they dislike. Then have one student explain the negative consequences if this responsibility is avoided and how others may react if they were made to take over this responsibility.

Responsibility Reaction
"Sentence Starters" Handout

In middle school, the biggest responsibility I have is . . .

In high school, the biggest responsibility I think I will have is . . .

After high school, I will have the added responsibility of . . .

In kindergarten my biggest responsibility was . . .

My teacher's biggest responsibility is . . .

My principal's biggest responsibility is . . .

If I could give away one responsibility that I have now it would be . . .

If my parents asked me to add a responsibility I would be willing to . . .

If I have a job, one major responsibility is to . . .

When I live on my own (away from my parents), my main responsibility will be to . . .

Being well mannered is a responsibility everyone has because . . .

Attitude is a part of responsibility because . . .

There is a time to give up a responsibility when . . .

I have the responsibility of meeting a schedule because . . .

Making good choices is my responsibility because . . .

If I make a promise, it is my responsibility to . . .

My responsibility(s) at home includes . . .

At school it is my responsibility to . . .

With friends I have the responsibility to . . .

Trust is a part of responsibility because . . .

It is my responsibility now to set a goal because it will help me . . .

Honesty / integrity is a part of responsibility because . . .

Responsibility takes courage when . . .

Responsibility requires dependability because . . .

Date_____

Dear Parent/Guardian:

Wow -- our students have really enjoyed internalizing individual responsibilities through a cooperative, team play known as "Responsibility Reaction!" Sentence starters such as "Making good choices is my responsibility because . . . " and "Trust is a part of responsibility because . . ." and others formed the basis for this activity in class today!

Questions at the end of the activity included, "Which responsibility(s) is the most difficult for you?" and "Do you feel it is easier to handle your responsibilities now than when you were younger?", etc.

At home, it would be helpful if you sit down with your child to discuss his/her responsibilities. Listen . . . listen . . . to his/her ideas about these and then let him/her hear your ideas! Both will probably learn a lot about each other and the ideal is for the responsibilities to be taken more seriously and performed more consistently!

Sincerely,

_____

Equality/Tolerance of Self and Others

Objective

Students will:

✔ become more aware and accepting of differences within him/herself and others

Materials Needed

"Equality/Tolerance Cards"

Procedures

1. The leader will cut out the 30 "Equality/Tolerance Cards."

2. He/she will assign pairs within the classroom.

3. Each pair of students will be given one card.

4. The leader will give the class 10 minutes to discuss the good in each description (negative comments are not allowed).

5. Then each pair of students will stand and present to the class the good found in each word on their card. (If there is time for the other class members to add comments, please allow.)

Discussion Questions

1. Since we have discussed the positive comments in these words, some of which are completely opposites, why do you think middle school students are sometimes unaccepting of the differences within others?

2. After this discussion, do you feel you can be more accepting of your own differences? Others differences? Why or why not?

3. When you were in kindergarten, did you accept the differences in others more or less? Why do you feel this way?

4. As we grow and become more mature, do you think it will be harder or easier to accept the differences of others and yourself?

5. Do you feel differences in people make the world a better place? Why or why not?

Variations

- This would be an excellent Language Arts or Social Studies project. A comparison of the words in literary or historical persons could be an excellent higher level thinking essay, etc.!

- Have the student identify ways he/she is similar to others in the class.

- Have the student identify ways he/she is different from others in the class.

Equality/Tolerance of Self and Others
"Equality/Tolerance Cards"

Equality/Tolerance Cards	Equality/Tolerance Cards	Equality/Tolerance Cards
HOT	**COLD**	**SAD**
Equality/Tolerance Cards	Equality/Tolerance Cards	Equality/Tolerance Cards
GLAD	**TALK**	**QUIET**
Equality/Tolerance Cards	Equality/Tolerance Cards	Equality/Tolerance Cards
SHORT	**TALL**	**COLOR**
Equality/Tolerance Cards	Equality/Tolerance Cards	Equality/Tolerance Cards
HAIR	**ARTISTIC**	**ATHLETE**
Equality/Tolerance Cards	Equality/Tolerance Cards	Equality/Tolerance Cards
MATH	**WRITER**	**NEW**

Equality/Tolerance of Self and Others
"Equality/Tolerance Cards"

Equality/Tolerance Cards	Equality/Tolerance Cards	Equality/Tolerance Cards
OLD	**POOR**	**RICH**
PERSON	**HISTORY**	**NIKE®**
KMART®	**ANCESTORS**	**FRIEND**
NICE	**MEAN**	**HEALTHY**
SICK	**FANCY**	**PLAIN**

Date_____

Dear Parent/Guardian:

During pre-adolescence and adolescence, the idea of individuality begins to form. Many times students find it difficult to accept the differences within him/herself from his/her best friends. For example, at these tender ages, your child may feel he/she is the "only" one who has to study 2 hours each afternoon, or the "only" one who can't talk on the telephone more than 30 minutes per day, or the "only" one with chores at home, etc.

Today in class, our character activities involved both "Equality and Tolerance of Self and Others." Discussion questions included "why" each student felt some people are unaccepting of differences with others. The students reflected on their earlier years (around preschool and kindergarten) and how they felt about others' differences at that time in their lives.

The big question asked was, "Do you feel differences in people make the world a better place? Why or why not?"

As the parent(s), please discuss this with your child -- even the differences of the people within your family! It could prove invaluable to your child's outlook toward him/herself and others!

Sincerely,

_____

Trust Is A Must

Objective

Students will:

✔ recognize the personal benefits resulting from good character choices made which will allow others to trust him/her

Materials Needed

Notebook paper
180 Days of Character
by Donna B. Forrest, LPC (optional)

Procedures

1. The leader will allow students to share their ideas of what trust involves.

2. After a 5 minute discussion, the leader may wish to read a definition of trust from the dictionary.

3. If a copy of *180 Days of Character* is available, refer to pages 83-95 for thought provoking statements concerning trust.

4. Next, have the students respond to the following words in an open class discussion:
   Gossip
   Promise
   Carefree
   Helpful / Caring
   Forgetful
   Responsible
   Respectful (of self and others)
   Sincere

5. For classwork or homework, have each student write a short essay explaining how being trusted can help them at home and school, both now and during the next few years. (i.e., What do they want to be trusted for, with, etc.?)

Discussion Questions

1. After our discussion, and as you begin to think of what you will write, what changes might you have to make in your own life to be trusted more at home? At school?
2. Will these changes be easy or difficult? Why?
3. Explain the place of trust in our study of Character. How is it related and how does it benefit you in your relationships?

Variations

• Without giving names or relationships, a class setting can be a good place to allow open discussion of times students have been "let down" or have "let others down" and the after effects of this (i.e., lack of trust for a time, etc.). This can also be a good setting to discuss the results of untrustworthy actions (i.e., anger, resentment, hurt, etc.). This is an excellent lesson to discuss the treatment of others as we want to be treated ourselves!

• Have students add words that relate to trust to the list given in this lesson.

• Identify ways trust can be broken and how it can be repaired.

Date_____

Dear Parent/Guardian:

The concept of TRUST is a character trait that is so important to our students at this age! Each student needs to be able to have a trusted adult(s), friend(s), and family member(s) in order to feel secure in his/her own world! Also, each student needs to become more and more trustworthy in order to gain the freedom(s) desired as each one matures.

Therefore, today our character lesson involved the definition of TRUST, and responses to the relationship of TRUST to such words as gossip, promise, carefree, helpful/caring, forgetful, responsible, respectful (of self and others) and sincere!

For homework, your child has been assigned a short essay explaining how being trusted can help them at home and school -- both now and in the future!

This is an ideal time to discuss your perspective of trust and maybe some of your own life experiences pertaining to trust with your child! Thanks for reinforcing this important character concept at home!

Sincerely,

_____

Copyrighted Attitudes

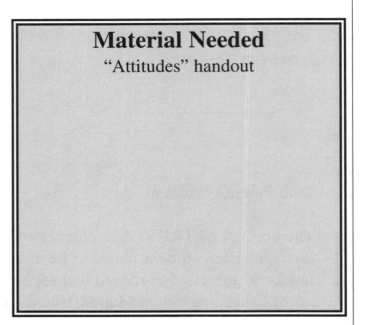

Objective

Students will:

✔ recognize the relationship of a positive attitude with success in a variety of settings

Material Needed

"Attitudes" handout

Procedures

1. The leader will introduce the following words: (write on one side of the board)
   "Go Team!" (said like a cheer!)
   Yes!
   A smiling face!
   A pat on the back!
   Thank you – you're really special!
   I'll do better next time!
   I'm down, but not out!
   I'm crushed (hurt), but not broken (won't give up)!
   I like you, but I don't like your actions!

2. Have the class respond to these "positive attitude" statements and the effects of such statements to people around.

3. Next, ask the students to think of negative statements they have heard recently. The leader will write these on the other side of the board.

4. Contrast and compare the effects of the positive and negative statements on success and/or failure.

Discussion Question

After the completion of the "Attitudes" handout the leader will (without allowing students names to be given), give some random responses for the class to decide how best to help each other become more positive. For example, if the response is positive, the class can confirm and offer even more positive statements. Or, if the response was passive or negative, the class can offer suggestions that might be more positive for that person.

* This is also an ideal time for the leader to recognize students who may have low self esteem and need some individual or small group attention. If the leader is a teacher, those student(s) might need to be referred to the school counselor.

Variations

- As a project (either individual or group) have the students research famous quotes that have to do with positive attitudes and bring to class for extra credit!
- Discuss body movements in relation to attitudes.
- Define and discuss *optimis*m and *pessimism.*

Copyrighted Attitudes
"Attitude" Handout

1. Think about the person(s) you know with the best attitudes. Explain what they have in common.

   _____

   _____

   _____

2. In what ways do you show your most positive attitudes?

   _____

   _____

   _____

3. In what ways do you show your most negative attitudes?

   _____

   _____

   _____

4. How are the responses from others (at home or school) different toward you when you show those positive attitudes (in #2 above) or those negative attitudes (in #3 above)?

   _____

   _____

   _____

5. Explain how these attitudes may or may not affect your middle and high school years!

   _____

   _____

   _____

6. What does the statement "Today is the first day of the rest of your life", have to do with attitude?

   _____

   _____

   _____

Date_____

Dear Parent/Guardian:

As adults we realize the importance of a positive attitude in our relationships with others at home and at work. For our students' developmental level, this needs to be taught and reinforced in order to help them become more aware of the effects of positive attitudes on their successes! As it has been said many times -- it's a much happier time when our glass is 1/2 full than when it is 1/2 empty!

Students in class today were given examples of positive statements and then were asked to think of negative statements to contrast. The comparison of the effects of each were discussed and some famous quotes about positive attitudes were shared.

As the parent, if you are aware of any positive quotes and can share them with your child so he/she can share with the class, please do so! With improved attitudes, life at home and school will become more improved and your child will definitely benefit!

Sincerely,

_____

Character Mold

Objective

Students will:

✔ consolidate the ideas taught in this chapter in order to define the type of character traits he/she wants to consciously work to improve in his/her personal life

Materials Needed

Plain paper (for cover and back of project)
Notebook paper (if students do not type)
Character Under Construction
by Donna B. Forrest (optional)

Procedures

1. The leader will review the major character traits discussed in this unit.
   Courage
   Respect
   Responsibility
   Equality / Tolerance
   Trust
   Attitude
   The character traits defined in the 1st lesson.

2. The leader will challenge the students to complete a three part project following the suggested outline below.

   I.   What I have learned from this character study
        My strong character traits
        My weak character traits
   II. Affects of my character on my own life
        Current
        Future
        Home
        School and/or Work
   III. Affects of the character of people around me (peer group, etc.) on my character and my personal ability to choose (saying yes, no, not for me, walking away, etc.)

3. It would be good to include in this project a unique cover page (art work, computer generated, etc.), and a dedication page (to meaningful people with good character modeling).

Discussion Questions

1. How can this project benefit you?
2. Some character traits other than those listed above are fairness, honesty, compassion/kindness, manners, goal setting, dependability. How you could you include these in your project?
3. Is there any person(s) you wish to share this project with?

Variations

- Poetry could be assigned to include character traits.
- A mentoring program for middle school students to perform raps, poetry, or read character literature to elementary students could be set up between the middle and elementary schools in a close area. (Ideas for this can be found in *Character Under Construction* by Donna B. Forrest, LPC.)
- Have the students name and list other character traits not discussed in this unit but that are important and tell "why."

Date_____

Dear Parent/Guardian:

As a completion to our character unit study, a review of the major character traits have been discussed in class today. These included courage, respect, responsibility, equality/tolerance, trust, and attitude.

A three part project following a given outline has been assigned to each student in order to compile his/her own character profile. Encourage your child to make this project a top priority and to keep it to review annually as a reminder through these important formative years of his/her "Character Mold"! All of us need reminders and sometimes to re-prioritize our own character -- this can really help as our students travel through developmental milestones that prepare them for adulthood!

Thank you so much for your support in this unit and in your child's character! Our hope is that this curriculum has reinforced the life skills you wish for your child to achieve!

Sincerely,

_____

Chapter 8

Career/School-to-Work Awareness

*"The only limit to our realization of tomorrow will be our doubts of today.
Let us move forward with strong and active faith."*
- Franklin Delano Roosevelt

Adolescents sometimes are shocked at the sudden realization that in a few short years a career must be chosen that will affect both their futures and lifestyles! All of a sudden, the reason for academics can become more relevant to each student internally. This unit will focus on activities to make career choices more individually real and important.

Goals -- both short and long -- can be set and, as a follow-up to the unit on character traits. Goals can become real with the help of a trusted adult family member or school staff member!

The exposure to various careers, educational requirements, and the relationship to self will, hopefully, will prove to be an invaluable unit of study!

The "ME" Life Research Project

Objective

Students will:

✔ implement a personal search as to his/her likes, dislikes, talents, special interests, etc. in order to become aware of the type of work that might be enjoyable over a life span.

Material Needed

"'ME' Life Research Project" handout

Procedures

1. The leader will prepare a discussion about the relationship of personal likes/dislikes that need to be considered when planning a career.

2. Students should be asked to volunteer any career they have considered pursuing. An example might be a student who comments they want to be a veterinarian because he/she likes animals.

3. The leader could ask the class to brainstorm what that career involves other than the fun part of being with animals. Answers could include educational requirements, long hours, physical requirements, medical situations involving surgeries, etc.

4. The leader could work through this with the class for various careers (be sure to include careers that do not involve college training).

Introduce the "'ME' Life Research Project" handout as a self-worksheet to begin looking at the relationship between individual traits and careers.

Discussion Questions

1. What new thoughts did this lesson bring to your mind concerning your future plans in relation to a career?
2. Who will you talk to or shadow at work in order to gather more information on certain careers discussed?

Variations

- Speakers from various careers discussed could be brought to class one time per week for a series of career awareness activities.
- A career assessment could be given to each student and the results discussed by the teacher or school counselor.
- The librarian could assist students in using career guides available in the school library to help with this lesson as well as the following ones in this unit.

The "ME" Life Research Project
"'ME' Life Research Project" Handout

I like to:	I do not like to:	SPECIAL THOUGHTS
I am good at (talented):	I cannot:	
My hobby(s) include:	In my spare time I would never:	
For a job I think I might like to:	For a job I know I could never:	
Education I might need:	After high school I am willing to go to school how many more years:	
People I could talk to about the jobs I mentioned:	People I could "shadow" at work:	
Why school is important NOW in considering jobs:	The number of years I have before finishing high school and making a decision about going to work or college:	
Miscellaneous thoughts about my future (positive)	Miscellaneous thoughts about my future (a little frightening)	

Date_____

Dear Parent/Guardian:

Today your child began to research various careers. The awareness of these careers combined with each individual student's likes and dislikes will begin to help students internalize personal goals for the future!

Please begin talking with your child about his/her thoughts. It is important to listen . . . listen . . . listen! Also, realize these goals may change many times over the next few years, but a constant review and revision of his/her goals will serve as an important motivational tool in the educational process.

Thanks for your support and help with this very important unit of study!

Sincerely,

_____

Choices

Objective

Students will:

✔ become more aware of the reason for doing his/her best in Middle School both through good character and the best possible performance academically.

Materials Needed

Technical School, Industry Apprenticeships, College – Handbooks
Speaker – High School Career Guidance Counselor (Optional)

Procedures

Set up: About 3 weeks prior to teaching this lesson, each student should write a school (technical or college) or industry requesting information on requirements to enter the educational or apprenticeship program(s) offered. This should be done with the leader present (possibly in the school library) in order to research and find proper addresses, etc.

1. After information is gathered, have students classify and group information into sections (i.e., technical schools – courses of study offered, industry – apprenticeships offered, etc.)

2. Allow the class to discuss, with the leader as the facilitator, the various information (this may take 2-3 class periods).

3. Have the students relate their academic and character performances in middle school to their future careers.

Discussion Questions

1. During this study, what was the most surprising fact(s) revealed concerning your preparation for the years following high school?
2. What did you learn that was the most encouraging? What was the most discouraging? Why?
3. Who can you talk to in order to begin setting a realistic career goal for yourself?

Variations

- Have an administrator talk to the class about possible clubs, school related responsibilities, etc. that might enhance each student's preparation (i.e., "Character Club" could sponsor a career "Application" or "Interview" Day where these skills can be taught on how to find a job.)
- Plan one or two field trips to a technical college and/or 4 year College.
- Order a PR video from several colleges and technical schools to be shown to the class.

Date_____

Dear Parent/Guardian:

As a continuation to our career awareness unit, various future educational and career choices available to each student are being studied. Some surprising and informative information has been gathered which is exciting to our students!

Through this study we have identified some adults that can help each student in setting realistic career goals. You are needed to identify other adults who can assist your child in this area. Possibly other family members, neighbors, or friends would be willing to help point out more choices than the ones we have covered in class!

Thank you for your interest in reinforcing choices that are available to each student through both educational and career options.

Sincerely,

_____

Guess What I Do

Objective

Students will:

✔ become more aware of the personalities and interests of people in various careers

Material Needed

"Career Cards"

Procedures

1. The leader will begin to give the clues from the "Career Card."

2. After those have been completed each student will be asked to write a description of a job for other class members to guess.

3. Discuss the following after each card is read and guessed:
   Education requirements
   Working with or away from people
   Inside or outside work required
   Physical ability and/or strength required
   Work for a company, school, or self owned business

Discussion Questions

1. Were there any areas discussed that you know you cannot consider for a career? Why?
2. Are there careers you would like to pursue, but have some doubts that it would be possible (i.e., finances, ability, etc.)? Explain and distinguish reality vs. fears.

Variations

- Have the school counselor come in after this lesson and discuss any career assessments available to the middle school students. It is possible that the counselor would have availability to individual assessment tools that each child could be given and results could be interpreted by the counselor.
- A personality inventory could be administered.
- A review of the permanent record of each student could be done to point out strong academic areas.

Guess What I Do

"Career Cards"

Guess What I Do Career Cards

I get to school before any child. I clean, wash, and prepare for every child and staff member in the school. Once I have done my job I get to leave before the afternoon buses! (lunchroom worker)

Guess What I Do Career Cards

No matter what the weather, I must be on the job. I get my work from the main office each morning. Once I leave I must continue delivery until it is complete. I had to pass a test to get my job. (mail carrier)

Guess What I Do Career Cards

I draw plans for large and small buildings and houses. I had to go to college longer than four years. I can either work for a large company or own my own business. (architect)

Guess What I Do Career Cards

I like working with numbers and have always enjoyed Math. Many businesses and individuals come to me to do their taxes. I finished college and had to pass an exam. (accountant/CPA)

Guess What I Do Career Cards

Since I enjoy helping and listening to children and teens, I chose a career that required 4 years of college and graduate school. I get to work in classrooms and with individuals. (guidance counselor)

Guess What I Do Career Cards

I like to travel to different places. It is fun to meet people from all walks of life when I travel. I enjoy meeting deadlines and the feeling of accomplishment. I had special training and passed a road test. (truck driver)

Guess What I Do Career Cards

I like being outside and watching things grow. I like nature and the smell of the earth. It is a good feeling to gather things that have grown and distribute them to various places all over the country. (farmer)

Guess What I Do Career Cards

Dogs are great to work with, but I could never watch them suffer so I cannot be a vet. It is fun to teach them to perform helpful tasks for elderly or physically challenged people so I decided to be… (dog trainer)

Guess What I Do Career Cards

I like the feeling of accomplishment when I am able to help someone pick out the vehicle of his/her choice and within the limits of what he/she can afford. (car salesman)

Guess What I Do Career Cards

I like to fill the medicine prescriptions that the doctor orders for people who are sick. I had to go to college about two extra years and take an exam. (pharmacist)

Guess What I Do Career Cards

Working with computers was always a hobby growing up. Then I decided I liked to build them and troubleshoot when repairs are needed on the computers. (computer engineer)

Guess What I Do Career Cards

I have strong convictions about right/wrong and love working within the government system. I must be elected by the people in the state to lead the state. (governor)

253

Date_____

Dear Parent/Guardian:

We are continuing to review various careers. Today we included educational requirements of some, whether the job requires working with or away from people, whether the work is inside or outside, and the physical ability and/or strength that may be required.

Also, we discussed benefits and limitations for working with a company versus self-employment. Of course, this is an overview and we have not gone into great detail. However, each student would grow from learning your opinion(s) as his/her parent on the above issues. Possibly you and/or a grandparent could share some experiences that may help your child understand the long term effects of choosing a career that requires certain abilities.

If you would like to talk to our class about your career, please let me know. As we continue this unit, your input would be appreciated!

Sincerely,

_____

Interviews With the Best

Objective

Students will:

✔ learn about various types of work

Material Needed

"Interview Questionnaire" handout

Procedures

1. The leader will discuss good interview manners such as asking politely if the person will spend 15 or 20 minutes to help complete an assignment for school. Also, the interview does not have to include a name if the person prefers.

2. The leader will give students one week to find and interview a family member or close friend.

3. On the due date, the leader will allow a 15 minute class discussion of the reactions to the interviews.

4. Then, an essay will be completed by each student with his/her personal reactions to the interview he/she conducted.

5. Follow-up comments by the leader on these reaction papers might be helpful to the student.

Discussion Questions

1. Did you get the impression that the person you interviewed liked going to work each day? Why or why not?

2. As the class discuss the interviews, what common factors seem to be present when the adults first chose their professions? Was there any unusual factor that you heard an adult comment on when choosing his/her profession?

3. What is the most important thing for you to consider as you choose your profession (i.e., money, hours to work, fulfillment, etc.)?

Variations

- Take these same interview questions, but limit the interviewee's ages to 50-65 and discuss the different options available in the world of work today (i.e., technology choices, etc.)!

- Interview a young adult who has only worked in his/her career less than 10 years - note the differences.

- Interview two people who work in the same type career and compare and contrast their comments.

Interviews With the Best
"Interview Questionnaire" Handout

1. At what age did you begin working? _____

2. What was your first job? _____

3. Did you like it? Why or why not? _____
_____
_____

4. How long have you worked in the job you are in now? _____

5. What is your current occupation? _____

6. Why and how did you choose this job? _____
_____
_____

7. How much education did you have to receive before taking this job? _____
_____

8. What do you like about this job _____
_____
_____

9. What do you dislike about this job? _____
_____
_____

10. Would you please take this time to give your best advice to me as I set future goals for myself and attempt to choose a career I will enjoy? _____
_____
_____

THANK YOU VERY MUCH!

Date_____

Dear Parent/Guardian:

Our students have enjoyed interviewing people in various careers over the last week. If you participated, we truly appreciate your input.

If you could possibly take your child to visit the person interviewed for part of a day to "shadow" and view the person actually at work, this could serve as a great learning tool! If not the person interviewed, possibly another person in a similar career could be observed.

Please discuss with your child what he/she learned from this interview and the others that have been orally discussed in class today! Thank you very much.

Sincerely,

_____

Jobs and Finances

<table>
<tr><td>

Objective

Students will:

✔ be exposed to "gross" salary versus "take home" pay and how to record deposits and expense into a checkbook register

</td><td>

Materials Needed

Calculators (optional)
Checkbook register
(copy one page for each student)

</td></tr>
</table>

Procedures

1. The leader will set up a part-time job scenario for the class. This could include a student who bags groceries locally 20 hours per week at $5.00 per hour.

2. A grocery store manager could be invited into the classroom to actually discuss duties, hours for part time students, and pay.

3. On the board the leader could show the following that might be deducted from the pay before it is given to the worker:

Gross (total pay)	=	$100.00 (20 hrs. X $5.00/hr.)
Social Security	=	? (figure at current rate)
Federal taxes	=	? (use tax table from CPA)
State taxes	=	? (use tax table fromCPA)
Misc. deductions	=	?
NET PAY	_____	(ACTUAL $ TAKEN HOME!)

4. Finally, the leader will show the class how to record a deposit into a checkbook and talk about expenses (such as gas to and from work, meals, etc.) and show the class how to keep a checkbook balanced.

Discussion Questions

1. What have you learned from this early working experience?
2. How much of your NET pay should you plan to save for emergencies? Why?
3. Should you keep a file with records of your pay? Why?

Variations

- A follow-up lesson with a mini budget could be set up and planning for emergencies implemented or saving for an item could be planned!
- Other local part-time jobs could be discussed and pay researched in order for students to compare their options.
- A sample of "how" to keep files with records of income and expenses could be set up within the class.

Date_____

Dear Parent/Guardian:

Today your student learned about a part-time job situation. Our class set up a proposed budget considering the suggested pay per hour less taxes and other deductions. Gross versus Net pay was explained. Wow – the students really were surprised in some areas!

If you know of a business that hires part time high school and/or college students, share that with your child so he/she might add that to our local possibilities of places of part-time employment. Even if your child is not of age to work yet or you are not ready for he/she to attempt a part-time job, this lesson should make earning and spending money more realistic.

Thank you for your input and follow-through at home.

Sincerely,

_____

Jobs and Emotions

Objective

Students will:

✔ become aware of the importance of cooperation, patience, tolerance of others, respect, responsibility, and emotional control in the world of work

Materials Needed

List of various jobs (student originated)
"Feeling" word list on chalkboard

Procedures

1. On one side of the board the leader will list feeling words such as (but not limited to) happy, satisfied, sad, angry, excited, apathetic, controlled, out of control, aggravated, pleased, etc.

2. On the other side of the board the leader will ask the students to give some careers they have considered pursuing in the future.

3. The leader will choose three of these to discuss in class. If possible, one career would involve working alone most of the day (i.e., computer data entry, researcher, etc.); one career would involve some interactions with others (i.e. accountant, etc.); and one career would involve constant contact with people – both employees and the public (i.e., bank manager, nurse, etc.).

4. Discuss a typical day on the job. Highlight some rewarding feelings and possible frustrations (i.e., personality differences among workers, etc.) The leader can describe situation(s) that may involve anger.

5. Next, personal plans should be discussed such as to "how to" handle these frustrations in order to personally do his/her job regardless of others.

6. Finally, have the students divide into groups to role play these situations.

Discussion Questions

1. Do you now, or have you had to deal with similar situations in school? Explain.
2. How would the consequences in school be similar or different to the consequences at work (both the good and bad)?
3. Why should you have a plan for handling your emotions at school and work?

Variations

- Choose a career that involves working with many people in various capacities such as industry, hospital, school, etc. Divide the class into groups and have each group write a 10 minute play to perform which exhibits at least 4 emotions – both good and not so good!

- Art classes could draw emotional exchanges on the job and exhibit them in the hallways!

- Interviews with people who have worked similar jobs could be done and their replies concerning emotions they have had to deal with shared with the class.

Date_____

Dear Parent/Guardian:

Today our students became more aware of the effects of emotional stability in the world of work. In our previous units we have covered responsible behaviors, grief and loss, anger, conflict resolution, and character traits. In this final unit on career awareness all these lessons combine and the individual's emotional component cannot be left out of his/her success in the future.

Everyone – young and old – experience good and bad days along with good and bad relationships. However, the older one becomes, the more we realize the importance of maintaining our own emotional composure!

Plans of how to maintain such composure were discussed and role played in class today. Please listen as your child describes this and watch for areas you may want to have input in helping to enhance this lesson!

Sincerely,

_____

Jobs in 2030

Objective

Students will:

✔ learn the impact he/she may have on the future of the world as a result of the education now being obtained

Materials Needed

Occupational Handbook or
Career Listing
Notebook paper
pen or pencil

Procedures

1. The leader will ask students to choose a career already discussed in this unit.

2. The student will write some facts about that career.

3. Next, the student will brainstorm and write "how" that career may change over the next 20-30 years. For example, houses may be built with stronger, different materials or cars may become smaller, larger, use less gas, or become electrical.

4. Then have the student write what old jobs might no longer be needed and what new jobs may result from these changes.

5. Finally, the student will summarize how his/her education of today will impact his/her future career when considering the changes that may take place.

Discussion Questions

1. How have jobs changed over the last 10 years?
2. What type jobs did your grandparents do to earn a living?
3. How were those jobs different in the past from similar jobs today?
4. What impact could your current education have on you 5 years from now ... 10 years from now ... when you are 50 years old?

Variations

- Bring in several grandparents to speak to the class about their careers and try to correspond by bringing in several parents who work in similar careers currently. Have the students compare and contrast the differences that have occurred in these two generations.
- Schedule several recent college and technical school graduates to speak to the class (in a forum style) about the jobs they found available upon graduation, type skills needed, etc.
- The students could write newspaper articles on future careers to submit to the school or local paper!

Date_____

Dear Parent/Guardian:

Our career lesson today proved to be quite exciting! Students were allowed to predict possible jobs that may be needed during the next 20-30 years and how these may differ from jobs available today! This was very interesting from your child's point of view!

With your life experiences and those of your parents, please discuss the changes that you have witnessed and/or heard about in various careers over the past 20-30 years (for example media and/or computer jobs, farming, etc.). The comparison will help your child realize the impact of his/her education today in preparing for the future changes that may be required in the world of work!

Sincerely,

_____

My Personal Plan

Objective

Students will:

✔ complete a 4 part project with goals outlined and strategies for attaining their goals included

Materials Needed

3 ring binder
Notebook paper

Procedures

1. The leader will explain the 4 parts of this project which are:
   -Current year
   -High School plan
   -Post High School plan
   -Desired career focus (List at least 6 possible jobs with as many different educational plans as possible. For example, some may require technical college, 4 year college, post graduate work, etc.)

2. The student will be assigned one part of this project per day. The first day the student will list goals for the current year and how he/she plans to attain these goals.

3. The second day the student will set goals for his/her high school career (academic, athletic, musical, artistic, etc.).

4. The third day the student will write plans for after high school and how he/she plans to follow through. Be sure that the student includes the impact of the first two parts on the third part which gives this project the "building effect."

5. Finally, the student will complete the 4th section by listing 6 possible jobs that he/she might enjoy (after being involved in the previous lessons of this unit). These should include at least 2 educational levels. For instance some could include a high school diploma, others a technical school, and others a 4 year college diploma, etc.

6. This project can have art work on the cover, etc. to emphasize the importance of formulating "plans" in life!

Discussion Questions

1. What have you learned about yourself from completing this project?
2. Where do you plan to keep this project and when should you plan to review and possibly revise your plan to fit your needs?
3. Why is it important to begin forming life "plans" as early as middle school?

Variations

- Have a section to list accomplishments/goals already attained in his/her life!
- Have the children take the projects home, go over them with his/her parent(s).
- Ask the school counselor to review the projects with each child as a form of encouragement!

Date_____

Dear Parent/Guardian:

As the final lesson in the Career Unit of study, your child has developed a personal folder with his/her goals in 4 parts. These are current goals, high school goals, plans for after high school, and possible careers that may be of interest.

Please review and discuss this with your child annually! As he/she matures these goals may need to be modified many times, but the initial plan is a starting point for your child to look into his/her own future and begin processing what "might" work for them as individuals!

Thank you for your support in this unit of study!

Sincerely,

_____

References

Barlett, John (1980). *Familiar quotations.* Boston, MA: Little, Brown and Company, Inc.

Forrest, Donna B. (1998). *180 days of character.* Chapin, SC: YouthLight, Inc.

Forrest, Donna B. (2000). *Character under construction.* Chapin, SC: YouthLight, Inc.

Moorefield, Story (1984). Handling stress in children. *The National Association of Elementary School Principals, 3,* 2.

Woolfolk, Anita E. (1995). *Educational psychology.* Boston, MA: Allyn & Bacon.